WORDS

AND OTHER WEAPONS

A Collection of Essays and Short Stories

By Thembe Khumalo

First published in Great Britain in 2023 by:

Carnelian Heart Publishing Ltd
Suite A
82 James Carter Road
Mildenhall
Suffolk
IP28 7DE
UK

www.carnelianheartpublishing.co.uk

Paperback ISBN   978-1-914287-44-2
eBook ISBN   978-1-914287-45-9

A CIP catalogue record for this book is available from the British Library.

The essays in this collection are from the author's perspective, and they have represented events as faithfully as possible. The short stories in this collection are entirely a work of fiction. The names, characters and incidents portrayed in it are the work of the author's imagination. Any resemblance to actual persons, living or dead, is purely coincidental.

Editors:
Lazarus Panashe Nyagwambo &
Samantha Rumbidzai Vazhure

Cover design & Layout: Brandbuilder Africa

Typeset by Carnelian Heart Publishing Ltd
Layout and formatting by DanTs Media

For Zahra and Nia and all the daughters of African women.

Table of Contents

THIRD PARTY

It's confirmed. My husband has brought a third party into our relationship.

When I first hear the news, I feel myself in free fall. You know that feeling when you seem to be sitting quietly in a chair, but really you are tumbling, somersaulting, carried on a jet stream. You are spinning, dizzy, ears blocked, eyes teary in the wind, with no idea where you will land or how. That was me. I was looking at my husband, floating beside me, and wondering how long we would be falling, like skydivers, flying, clutching one another, sometimes breaking.

Sometimes something bad seems worse at first. Later, when you have more information, you are relieved, and you relax. I didn't know if that would be us. If we would land on goose-down bedding, softly plopping, sighing, giggling, saying whew that was quite a ride, it gave us such a fright.

Other times the bad news is better at first, and then bad again, or worse. Your fall becomes like trampolining, bouncing, landing then up high again, never sure if the horror has ended. I wondered if this would be us.

Sometimes the bad news is just a big hole in the surface of your quietly contented life. Like a fall in which you land on rock or tarmac, jarring, bodies crunching. Things just bad. "Banish the thought!" I tell myself. We will be ok. We have to be ok.

But between the news and becoming ok, there is a whole country which we must traverse. This is the journey that no one can walk for you; the endless road that stretches out before us.

I love to look at my husband. The day we met at a friend's house after more than twenty years of passing hellos, the night I watched him like a blockbuster movie I had not got round to seeing the first time around, I went home and texted my girlfriend to say I had met "a ridiculously good-looking man". This is how I view him still. And so, I love to look at him as he goes about his business, just drinking in the visual delight of him.

But after the news, I am looking at him differently now. I am no longer looking at him for pleasure, like a piece of art. Now I am looking at him to read him, like a complicated book in a foreign language. I want to decipher what is written on his face and in his eyes. I want to understand where on the barometer of fear he currently is, so that I can take my cue from him and meet him there. I want to talk him down if the reading is too high, or to say, actually, this is somewhat serious, if he appears too nonchalant.

At first, he is neither too worried nor too blase; not too hot and not too cold. Like Goldilocks' porridge, he is just right; just his usual self: calm and quite matter of fact about the fraying at the edges of our happy life. His reaction is adult and honest and I love him for it. I am filled with calm confidence that we will overcome this pesky obstacle that I have started to think of as Mr O.

But then the pressure mounts, and then he is shaken, and then so am I. And the more the matter is talked about, the more consultations are made, the more real it becomes. The reactions of those around us cover the full spectrum, from utterly bewildered, burn the house down emotional exhibitions, to hurling of prayers and worries and words of affirmation, to denial and disbelief. We see it all. We wonder. We are drawn in sometimes, and other times we are dismissive. We marvel at it all.

In the meantime, our third party goes everywhere with us. At this stage, Mr O is easy to ignore. He doesn't make a fuss or unduly draw attention to himself. But we know he is there, my husband and I. And I wonder whether he is as present for him as he is for me. My children had a sports coach called Mr O once. He was a nice guy; not like this Mr O, who is very quiet, but somehow threatening, malevolent.

There is a brown envelope at the bottom of our bed. It is marked "FOR THEMBE" in black square capital letters. It is for me. But it is not about me. It contains pictures and notes about Mr O and his relationship with my husband. It holds the damning evidence that has come to shake our house. We have only been married for a year. We are still in the process of becoming an us.

Sometimes at night when this man I love is trying to annihilate his reality with other peoples' realities on CNN, or escaping into made up worlds on Netflix, or keeping track of details that are fun to keep track of (not like the details in the brown envelope) by watching sports commentary, I think about Mr O. Sometimes when I put my head on my husband's chest, I have silent conversations with Mr O. I ask him why he is in our lives, what his game plan is. I am always careful to be polite – I would hate to awaken anything sinister in him or make him angry in any way. I respectfully enquire about his life purpose and his goals; I ask him what he came to teach us. The conversations are only slightly different from the ones I have with my coaching clients. Except that Mr O doesn't answer.

I have to believe that what we have so far will be enough to sustain us; that the house we've built in just three years of loving and one year of marriage is strong enough to shelter us wholly in this season and beyond; that love and faith will cover us; that laughter will soothe and maybe even medicate us; that relaxed respect will reward us all the way. I have to believe. I have to receive.

"How are you?" the people are asking. How am I? Well, I am not the one you need to worry about, but since you ask, I am a little dizzy. Saltwater wells in my mouth. Oh, is it nausea? No, it's fear.

I go about my business, reminding myself that I have no business feeling destabilised or discombobulated. I scold and reprimand myself with reminders that I am not the one who is literally joined at the hip to Mr O. I am not the one who will be losing an organ in the next few weeks. I am not the host of an oncocytoma.

We went to a party this weekend; me, my husband, his kidney and Mr O. Four of us, but only taking up two seats. While it looks like Mr O is only taking up the small space on the inside, the space against the kidney which must now lay down its life for him, the truth is, he takes up much more than that. He consumes our waking moments and our conversations. He takes up space in our quiet time, in our together time and in our alone time. He is a silent guest at every meal, as I observe food groups being consumed, as I interpret them for poisons that might possibly nourish Mr O. Will he grow, will he turn out to be nasty, will he suddenly reveal roots and branches that could not be seen on the pictures in the brown envelope?

We don't know. We don't know and in not knowing there is no peace for us. In the bed we share with him there is not much rest for us.

And so, I do my work. I run. I walk the dog and text the kids. I bake. I keep myself busy.

Mr O and his companion too are doing their work; visiting doctors, having tests, getting to know each other better I suppose.

Nobody knows how a story will end until it is ended.

Our relationship with Mr O is not yet ended.

We ourselves remain unended.

LET US PRAY

Dear Mama

You and Baba taught me to pray when I was a little child. Before I even had a concept of who or what God was, you directed my path and chose Him for me; and you made sure that I chose Him for myself over and over again. It wasn't always easy to choose Him – because you didn't always make Him out to be a very nice guy. I think one reason He wasn't a preferred choice back then is I didn't feel like a good person. When I looked at God through your eyes, He seemed so rigid, harsh and inflexible. It seemed like He was just waiting for me to fail, to stumble, to show how bad I was so that He could bring out his array of punishments and retribution. He didn't seem much like a loving, kind or forgiving Father back then.

But now that I am older, I've figured out my own relationship with God, and it's a good one. I think He wants me to succeed, Mama. I think God wants to see me win. I think He is holding His breath for my next achievement, watching for me to turn my next corner of progress, to say my next 'No' to something that won't edify me, and to accept my next opportunity to shine. That's the kind of Father I think He is.

So I thought this year, as we're working on our resolutions, we could try something different. In the same way you taught me to pray all those years ago, how about I play the teacher? I'll try and show you a different way to pray, and I would like us to try my way just for this year. We can see how you feel at the end of it, and then decide if you want to go back to your usual way. But let's stick with it for a year, OK?

Mama when you pray for me this year, your prayers will only be prayers of joy. Joy and thanksgiving; that's how you'll pray for me, please.

When you pray for me this year, pray thanking God for all that I am. Say to Him, Father, that youngest one of mine, that one that's so like me and yet seems not to hear me when I speak? Say to Him, That's the one I want to thank You for.

Say, I thank You for her head, forever in the clouds, for the never-ending stream of ideas gushing out of there. I thank You for her radiant smile that shines like a beam of light and makes everybody want to be her friend. I thank You for her social skills that open doors for her that others find locked tight.

I thank You for the confidence with which she marches in where angels fear to tread. Her courage, which enables her to do the things that frighten most of us, to walk a different path and speak a different language, even one that no one understands. I thank You for her willingness to blaze those trails because Africa needs women who aren't trapped by social convention and are not held back by "what will people say". Say it Mama, I know it will seem strange to you to pray this way, but I also know that God will understand.

When you pray for me, don't pray in prophecy – predicting doom and damnation on account of my wicked ways, my errant heart, my stubborn soul. When you pray for me, don't pray in fear anymore, Mama. Don't talk to God about my kids and how much they need me. Don't tell Him they'll be orphans if I misbehave. Don't report on me to God because I drink wine and sometimes even come home after dark. Don't say to Him you think I might get AIDS or never make it into heaven because I am a fornicator because I befriend girls who wear too much makeup and whose trousers are too tight.

Don't worry God with these concerns – He knows so much more than you do, and guess what, He is OK with me. And I'm OK with Him. Don't tell God to protect me from myself and that my reputation is in jeopardy. God doesn't need you to say these things to Him regardless of their truth or lack thereof. He doesn't need your worry over my wretchedness. Mama, God doesn't deserve your disbelief in His capacity to make all things work together for good in my life.

God desires your praises concerning me, Mama. He desires your thanksgiving regarding all that I am, not just the parts that you agree with. God wants to hear you pray with joy. Pray for me Mama, please never stop praying for me.

But when you pray for me, pray with joy. Pray with thanksgiving.

While I am living here on earth, celebrate me to your God. And even when I am gone, if I should go before you, celebrate all that you knew of me. Infuse your prayers with joy and sing songs of gladness when you remember me.

God needs to hear you say how blessed you feel to have me for your child and not how much I worry you. He needs to know that you are not grumbling about the gift you have that is me. God, you see, is so much bigger than all the things that give you sleepless nights.

When you have prayed with joy for me, when you have mastered this style of conversation with your God, try praying for your other children the same way. My siblings too deserve to feel like they are a gift and a blessing when you pray. Try thanking God for every aspect of their character – even the aspects that confound you, Mama.

Pray for us with joy this year and let us see how God will answer.

I love you Mama.

I thank God for you.

WOMEN LOVE MEN

"Well," Thato began.

Immediately, she realised her mistake. Starting any proposition with "well" was certainly not a recipe for success. Mrs Pierce would have been very disappointed. She looked at the panel before her – serious, smart (supposedly) and well-meaning. She had started, so she might as well get on with it.

"In a vast majority of African communities," she picked up, careful not to generalise, "women love men. Women have sex with men. Women build families, homesteads and legacies with men."

She scanned the faces in front of her, hoping for a raised eyebrow, the beginnings of a smile, a slight change of posture to indicate a growing interest in what she hoped was her provocative opening. They had nothing for her.

OK. Dive right in then, she thought.

"It is therefore imperative that we look for a different language to describe our aspirations toward equality of the sexes. If we genuinely desire peace and prosperity for men and women alike; if our goal is to have harmony in homes and communities; if we aim to create empathy and understanding between men and women, then we need to change the language we use to describe this process of discovery."

She took a deep breath and waded forward.

"We cannot use the language of war to describe a process of creating agreement. We need to shift, not just our narrative, but our entire posture from warmongering to peace-building."

She knew she had gone out on a limb with the last statement, but it was do or die at this point. The essence of the research that she wanted to conduct was described in detail in the proposal. This interview was supposed to help her clarify any points of concern. The room was almost impossible to read. Except for one tiny twitch in the corner of the one woman's mouth.

"Miss Khabela." It was a complete sentence. A prison sentence if you will. One that would condemn her and her research to the massive archives of the unrealised ideas of the world. "Miss Khabela." She said it again for emphasis. "One does not end war by pretending it is a summer picnic. One does not tame a dictator by adjusting the narrative around him to accommodate his sensibilities. We need to confront patriarchy with boldness, not to tiptoe around it."

"Well, I'm not..." She was interrupting. And starting a sentence with that word again. A double whammy. It seemed she was intent on breaking all the rules she'd learnt in Mrs Pierce's English class. "I'm not suggesting that we should adjust to accommodate men's sensibilities. I'm saying both men and women would benefit from us making adjustments that demonstrate our search for cohesion rather than conflict. I'm suggesting…"

The dirty blonde returned the interruption favour. "Do you understand the numbers, Miss Khabela?" The way she asked made it clear that anyone who didn't understand the numbers was not worth entertaining. And she did not believe Thatho understood the numbers.

"Violence against women… the gender pay gap… the percentage of child abuse cases where men are perpetrators… We are interested in statistics, Miss Khabela, not semantics."

Cute, thought Thato. For someone who wasn't interested in semantics, that was a pretty cute closing.

The redhead on the end cleared her throat. Her face immediately flushed bright red from the pressure of making herself noticed. Thato could tell that getting comfortable with visibility was something she'd had to work hard at to be on this panel. But clearly, she needed more, because she was still managing to give off intern vibes.

"Your idea is quite original and commendable," she said, smiling encouragingly. The gesture seemed out of place since she was the one who actually required the most encouragement, but her training required it. "We just don't think…"

Did she just use the word 'we' followed by 'think'? What were they doing at this place, getting together for group thinking sessions?

"We don't think it would be fair," she continued, "to trivialise the plight of so many women who are genuinely suffering, so that we can accommodate the views of an elite few."

Ummm… first of all, you clearly haven't understood a thing I've said. Secondly, it's not about the views of an elite few, it's about the reality of almost all womankind. In fact, all women, except the tiny majority that are lesbian. It's men that women love, so why promote this enmity between them?

The redhead continued, her confidence boosted by the nodding heads of other members of the panel. Thato had already lost interest in what she was saying, so she focused instead on studying the speaker. Her teeth were crooked, which was very unsettling in a white person, because didn't they all get braces and emerge in the adult world with their teeth forcefully wired down in straight lines to ensure their fake smiles would seem benign?

She remembered as a child, being subjected to the kind of touristy scrutiny that was very common in the small missionary community that she grew up in, where the whites would gather groups of local children and proceed to run commentaries on them as if they were livestock.

"Look how beautiful their teeth are, Annabel," one would say to the other, "Like a straight row of mealies on the cob." And they would laugh delightedly, barely masking their envy.

Or "Look how shiny their skin is… I am told they polish it with coconut oil."

"Oh how very quaint," another would remark. "But I doubt they can afford coconut oil in these parts. It's most likely petroleum jelly."

And so they would continue until they got bored, or it was time for gin and tonics at the club, whichever came first.

The black guy was quiet.

Thato tried to imagine his dilemma. She recognised that supporting her and her proposition could be a career limiting move for him. Suggesting an end to war stories for someone who made a living as an arms dealer certainly would be counterproductive in the short run. But if anybody was thinking longer term, they would see at once what an important idea it was, not just in the conversation around gender in Africa, but in conversations on a range of subjects around the world – race, religion, economics.

However, as an African male, he was surely exhausted by the continued diatribes of the rabid feminists in his professional life? The same feminists that organisations like his funded. The same ones that vociferously declared one thing at work but went home to play out another. Because the challenges at work required them to toe the donors' line. Donors, or rather, funding partners as they were now called, as if to assuage the guilt that their interminable demands should have triggered. Funding partners liked their recipients to follow a certain rhetorical line. It was an important part of building credibility for the causes they funded.

The gender crowd liked to hear stories of staff members leaving marriages in which they didn't feel valued, or stories of conflicts with patriarchal fathers. They wanted to believe that their gospel was the primary diet on which the staff members subsisted, and the evidence of this was an important part of earning membership to the donor favourites club.

At home though, Thatho knew most of these so-called feminists didn't bother to try and live out the things they preached at work. Dumping a husband was a last resort in a society where a woman's worth was still measured by her capacity to manage a home and family; where her character was judged on the basis of her ability to seem disinterested in the opposite sex, and indeed sexual activity, unless it was within the confines of a respectable marriage union. A woman didn't easily move out of those confines once she was settled. In a country where women outnumbered men, and the scramble for husbands was a reality, you would be hard pressed to find a woman who let her feminist views get in the way of the title of "Mrs".

Eventually, he spoke. "Ms Khabela, there is no social science that suggests your ideas have enough merit to warrant the support we could offer. There is very little published on the subject and not much academic exploration. Given the many urgent and pressing needs that our agency has, I can't see us putting any resources behind something like this. It's an outlier."

She was impressed by the authority with which he spoke, taking charge of the conversation and making the two women beside him look redundant and somehow, not very smart.

How interesting, she thought. *Even here, the patriarchy is at work.*

Dirty blonde bristled. Clearly not happy to be upstaged by black guy, she needed to have the final word. After all, the money would be coming from her fellow countrymen, not his. Never mind that she had escaped the dreariness of Europe for the clashing scenes and sounds of Africa. Escaping the mediocrity of an unremarkable career in Bergen to come and occupy a position as little less than a minor god on a continent defined by how much aid would come its way every year, dirty blonde now controlled her own little piece of that life-giving aid. She needed Thato to know that. Thatho and black guy.

"Thank you, Ms Khabela," she said. It was the look, not the words, that told her she was dismissed.

As Thatho made her way to the door at a steady pace, not too rushed as if confirming the rejection and not too slow, suggesting she was resisting it, she suddenly remembered an incident where she'd been moderating a discussion about gender-based violence. She had asked the activists around the table when they had first perpetrated violence against a woman. They looked at her with a mixture of impatience and confusion. They weren't the enemy, didn't she understand that? They were the people who had come to fix the perpetrators who were obviously broken and needing repair.

She was accustomed to that look, but undeterred, she had pressed on, "What about your housekeeper," she asked, choosing not to use the more provocative "maid" that she knew everyone used outside the confines of donor-led discussions. "Have you ever dismissed a maid because she fell pregnant? Or denied her proper maternity leave and time to breastfeed?" There was a change in the posture of the activists. "As an elder family member, have you ever participated in sending a pregnant niece to a boy's home where you knew she wasn't wanted or welcome under the guise of culture?" They began to look uncomfortable.

"We have chosen to think about GBV as something that happens in other people's houses." She had told them. "But we too are perpetrators. And once we begin to see ourselves as perpetrators, we can begin to look differently at those we previously condemned; to see them as people after all – flawed, sometimes ignorant, often well-meaning people."

Thatho looked back into the room as she pulled the door open. Madam red hair was making copious notes in classic personal assistant pose. Black guy was on his phone already, and dirty blonde was staring straight at her with satisfaction, as if waiting to be congratulated for a job well done.

BLOOMING LIKE A FLOWER

Suddenly she is all sharp angles and long bones.

Suddenly also un-huggable and certainly not in that squishy squashy cuddlesome way of before.

Suddenly she is sassing me and answering back.

Not in that charmingly precocious way, but with a little venom on her tongue. Like a brat. Like a woman. Suddenly the years are upon us and a teenager is born.

When I brought her home at first, she was hardly there. My first, my only barely there person - my Daughter Won. The volume of paraphernalia ascribed to her – to her care, to her bathing routines, to her health, to her entertainment, to her advantageous development – in comparison to the space that she herself took up was just short of astounding. And she was so cuddlesome. And gorgeoulicious. And mine – or so I thought for a minute or two.

But she was always her own person and I learnt that lesson well. I never tried to make the mistake with Daughter Too

Then suddenly there were curves. Curves everywhere, along the long bones and in places, well… just everywhere. It was a sight to behold I tell you. There were boobs and buttocks and golden skin in tiny shorts and long long legs and arms and smiles. And crooked teeth were suddenly straight, and charm could be exuded when necessary.

And it was me. It was me she was smiling at. I had to look over my shoulder just to check. But there was no one else there. And I had to ask, is it me, is it me you are smiling at and me you are happy to see? Me? She laughed. She smiled and then she laughed again and she was still looking straight at me. And then she said, "Mom. You're so cute." And then I fell in love. Again.

Firstly, she was soft and fluffy with not enough hair and most of it not in the right places. And she was not a good-looking baby, but she improved with age, thank God.

And then she was an earnest only girl, playing alone, talking to stones and vegetables in the lonely garden. And then there was a baby sister – a person of her own. A soldier she could marshal, direct and cause to march. A pupil she could teach and train and teach and train again. There were years and years of that – of listening to them playing happily outside on a weekend afternoon as I took my nap. It was delicious, and divine.

And then the bitter twisted time that lasted but a moment. The time of mom you are too much in my life, and me aghast, bewildered. A time when baby sister sat bewildered saying "Mom she is so rude to you." Don't worry love, I say, it's just her hormones. A baby sister hopes she will never develop horrific hormones. But she does, and so the journey starts again. She enters the tunnel of adolescence. The dark and grumpy tunnel full of closed doors and silent sulks. The tunnel with its magical moments of open heartedness, of vulnerability, and pure unbridled love. We walk it together, the three of us, with smiles and scowls and questioning and continuous forgiveness.

And now she is on her way out. Now there is a golden season of a golden age. A girl with golden legs and shining eyes and diamond smiles. A long girl who loves me and oh how I am in love with her. Again and again. All over again.

WHERE DOES KHULU GO?

In this part of Africa, Khulu is a diminutive for a word that means elder father – *ubab'omkhulu*. It's what my siblings and I have learnt to call my father in the years following the arrival of grandchildren. Our parents went from Mama and Baba to Gogo and Khulu. They are an exemplary couple in so many ways, and even today their love and commitment, their loyalty and a sense of real partnership leaves many in awe. Many includes myself.

They set such a high standard for what marriage should look like, that as a young girl I was convinced I could never attain it – and so I wouldn't even try. I was a freshly baked pup straight out of private school, full of ideals of feminism and independence and changing the world and blazing a trail with my name on it – across oceans and continents and galaxies. I knew that to consider the concept of marriage would include things like compromise, concession and those were things I didn't want to do. I later did of course but that is not today's story.

In the years when we were growing up, my father was a dashing figure – years ahead of his time, full of wisdom and knowledge, quoting Shakespeare down the passage, and doing jumping jacks in the bathroom as part of his morning routine. He'd been among the first people in his community to earn a university degree and was always challenging us, musically, intellectually, spiritually. And then one day, my father was gone. Not gone as in dead gone, but gone just the same.

Five years before that, my parents lived an almost idyllic life for many retirees in Zimbabwe. All of their born children still alive, productive. All of their ten grandchildren, also alive and doing reasonably well. Themselves, able and energetic, brimming over with good health and Christian teaching; active members of a community in which they were held in high regard by many.

And then one day the call came while I was at work. It came early in the morning, and it came as a shock, because my parents were truly independent – they did not depend. But the call came, and I took it. "Your father is ill, my mother said." And I sat down and thought, "this is it."

But that wasn't it. I spoke to him myself that same morning. He sounded alright – a little embarrassed perhaps. It was merely a urinary tract infection. Antibiotic dispensed, life goes on. They reported at the end of that day after returning from the GP and test and pharmacy visits. I was relieved.

The next day my mother called again, "Something has happened to your father." Then I went home to Luveve.

I didn't want to believe or describe my father as having a mental illness, because, well, it sounds so pitiful. And I don't want him to be an object of pity. For so long respected and admired, that guy was ahead of his time in so many ways. But when a wound has affected your brain and only parts of it have recovered, what else can I call it. An illness, a mental illness.

When my parents woke up that morning, they had a chat. My mother tends to rise very early to pray for her children and do whatever else Gogos do at that hour. She went to the kitchen and made breakfast. When she came back to say to Khulu, do you want to come and eat with me or should I bring you breakfast in bed – a rare treat for such an active couple – my father was gone.

I mean, he was there – alive, but gone. He was incoherent. He had lost all control of himself. He couldn't speak. He couldn't recognise anyone. He couldn't remember anything, couldn't walk, couldn't follow a conversation or a written text. In the nightmare weeks that followed, we tried to make a connection between the illness the GP had diagnosed and what we could see with our eyes, and we couldn't, because there was no connection.

My father had suffered a bleed on his brain, and then Khulu was gone. Today he sits, he looks, but I am not sure what he sees. He cannot follow to read, to watch TV, to engage intellectually. And so he sits. Of all the heartbreaking things, this for me is the worst, and I wonder, where does Khulu go? Where does he go in the morning after he has done all that is normal? When they have bathed and shaved and groomed him, when the nurse has helped him eat his breakfast, and he is not yet ready for lunch, what follows in that gap?

There is nothing that follows. He just sits. In his mind, where does he go? What is the running script that accompanies us all as we go about our day, what does his say? Is it just silent in there?

This question disturbs and distracts me, pains and persecutes me, because I need to know where Khulu goes. Because how can someone be here but not be here? How can I lose my father while he lives?

I have asked myself many times why I need to know this, why it's so important to me. I think it's because if you are nowhere, then... well, you are no one. Someone can't be nowhere, someone must be somewhere.

I can't have Khulu not be anyone.

Because if he is no one, then who is Gogo?

And who am I?

TEARS IN MATABELELAND

I didn't get it at first. Didn't get how surviving this particular genocide would impose specific indelible markings on my character. There are deep deep markings – like scratches wrought on wood with a heavy metal object. They are not like the kind children leave when they come out of the bath and leave wet imprints on your wooden floor, or the kinds your helper makes on the tiles when she drags a piece of furniture instead of lifting it. These markings can't be polished away with a bit of tender love and care. These markings are like tribal tattoos, where the scars rise loud against the skin – proclaiming their ownership of you. They are deep. They are permanent.

I don't know who I might have been without the genocide, how I might have turned out differently, or how it has affected others who also survived it, but in completely different ways. When I joined a university class in Rwanda that included students from war-torn countries all over Africa, I began to comprehend how war just interrupts your normal life. How you can just be minding your business, being a family, following news on the radios and then... soldiers, hiding, running, packing, hurrying. Up until that point, I hadn't understood that refugee camps are full of people who were otherwise just like us, who'd been regular kids in regular families... Just like me.

But still, I hadn't thought of myself, my life, as being in any way like them or theirs. Hadn't seen the connection, not until now. Not until I started to understand that some of my ways are linked to childhood trauma, to living in an atmosphere filled with the tension of violence and pervasive constant fear at a young age.

Fear has always been my companion. I say always, because I don't really remember what I was like before the genocide, before I was fearful. There are photos of me at about three years old, smiling, clutching crusts of bread in chubby little fingers. Happy and fear free as only a three-year-old can be. In those photos, I could be anyone.

I was young when Zimbabwe became independent. I remember at eight years old standing with my father in the grounds of the teachers college where he presided as the principal, and watching the old Rhodesian flag come down and a new one go up. I remember him explaining to me how the country would be changing its name and how a war I had been barely aware of had ended.

That was the beginning of another war – a war of terror against a minority tribe. A war in which my mother's colleagues at the school in which she taught would promise her that they would watch the heads of people like us rolling in the street, that the heads would make a sound as they rolled, "*kunguru kunguru kunguru...*" down the roads. She would come home and share these stories with my father, and the terror would overflow onto us. I absorbed the fear of the adults around me as devoutly as I absorbed everything they taught about God and Jesus and the importance of doing well at school.

During the genocide, I learnt that I could get into trouble, very very big trouble, even if I hadn't done anything wrong. I learnt that a long flat box in which a mother housed a knitting machine could be a source of suspicion, because it was just the right size and shape to house a rifle. I learnt that a mother, alone with her daughters, her family incomplete, could try very hard to be very brave and her girls would still be enveloped in terror.

I learnt that a father could be sent away to work in another town, while his wife was posted elsewhere, even though they worked for the same government department. I later learnt that this could strategically aid the process of dismantling an ethnic group.

I learnt that horrors could be visited on a person, a family or a community without provocation; that if you were in your home minding your own business, and soldiers came in to search for dissidents and they found your father's sleeping bag and it happened to be army green in colour, this could be the beginning of a very bad conversation for you. Because how could a family in the townships, in Luveve, just happen to own a sleeping bag? What did township families know about camping and hiking and outdoor exploits?

I learnt that people who argued or answered back, or tried too hard to explain, or appeared to be proud, or thought they could use logic, or appeared to be too clever, people like this could be taken away and never come back.

I learnt to be afraid – properly, thoroughly, wholeheartedly afraid. I learnt to fear not just with my mouth and my mind, but with my whole body.

Years later, alone with my two little girls, post-divorce, I would relive the fears of my childhood as the same government shot protesters in the streets, or unleashed destruction on homes in the townships, or spouted violent rhetoric against the opposition party. I cannot say that the fear would return, because it has never left. But it would be amplified and burn like an ember doused with petrol, flames rising.

This fear would revisit me again and again in my adult life as *uvalo*. *Uvalo* is a Ndebele word meaning anxiety, fear, apprehension. It can also refer to the pit of the stomach or the cartilage at the bottom of the sternum.

The fear I was trained into during Gukurahundi is a scab that never quite became a scar. It lies dormant there for months or even years. It wouldn't matter how benign a matter was, and I had no way of knowing when it would turn up – a boss summons me to his office; an imperious in-law demands an audience, a throw-away remark about "*maNdevere*", and instant *uvalo* is activated. The system remembers – jaw locked, chest tight, breathing suspended. The engagement would be immediate, the overwhelm complete. There is nothing rational about that kind of fear.

***

More years later, I am sitting in a building in Bulawayo, part of a team that was hosting a dialogue event on transitional justice. Change is in the air across the country. Hope is palpable as the citizens rally for closure, for an end to unheard pain.

A tall, lean man is sitting with unquestionable dignity in his wheelchair. He gives the impression of having been folded over twice in order to fit into it. When he speaks, his voice is startlingly strong, belying his fragile physical presentation, and his message is clear as it rings across the room. He is unemotional as he recounts his story, but all around him, we are wiping our eyes. We are weeping.

This man, Councillor E Ncube, is just one of the people who participated in the Independent Dialogue on Transitional Justice held on Wednesday morning. Bulawayo delivered a warm sunny day in its usual fashion but within the walls of the Bulawayo Club, there was a chill in the air and pain was visible in the faces of people in the room.

At the top table, there are two empty chairs which should have been occupied by representatives of the ruling party and the main opposition. I take a couple of pictures of the empty seats. Ghost chairs, I think to myself with a chuckle. Then I realise it is these ghosts who are running the country, and my little private joke is not so funny anymore.

Proceedings open with various speakers giving an overview of the meaning of transitional justice and placing this into context in the Zimbabwean situation. They speak of accountability, truth telling and a victim-led process. These are things I have heard or read before over the years in conversations about the genocide, though I am one of thousands who wait to see them realised in Zimbabwe.

For me, the most depressing input of the entire conversation was the presentation made by the co-minister of National Healing and Reconciliation, a man called Moses Mzila Ndlovu.

Having pursued a career in Media and Communication, I have been a facilitator and MC at many events, from beauty pageants to business dialogues, from kitchen teas to training seminars. But I have never had to hand over the microphone to someone else because tears threatened to overwhelm me. Until this day.

The minister is frank and open about his role in the Government of National Unity. His presentation is largely the story of an abusive relationship. He speaks of how meetings between the organ and villagers are disrupted by police; of the contempt the law enforcement agents have for the process. He recounts a two-year long effort by the organ to get a meeting with the head of security, of which the process still has not yielded any success. The Minister closes by telling the audience in no uncertain terms that the Organ for National Healing and Reconciliation does not in fact have the power to implement a process of national healing or reconciliation, and that it has little or no real authority. The words which he repeats several times and which leave me desolate are, "We are emasculated."

I hate this word "emasculate" and I hate it all the more when I hear it spoken by a man, referring to himself. What he is in fact saying is, "We are rendered impotent, we have no power, we are made ineffective and invalid." I listen to this man and wish it was a third party describing these things, so that he, the government representative, would have the chance to argue, to explain or to rebut. But it is he himself, and so there is no one to disagree. The minister poses a question which no one can answer, "If you are emasculated and you are assigned to such an important task, then what do you do?"

A representative of ZAPU, the opposition party after the first elections, is scathing and unapologetic in his description of the Government of National Unity. His candid take on the role of certain government ministers is, "They are not honourable, but honorary ministers. They hold the title but have no ministerial powers." What he is describing is the same emasculation that the Minister talked about earlier.

He goes on to talk about the lack of trust in the police force, the apathy of cabinet ministers who have done nothing about the haphazard exhumations of victims of the genocide currently taking place, and the indignities of enduring poverty caused by other people's corruption. Of the

Government of National Unity itself, he says, "I see no unity... I see no government." At some point in his presentation, this gentleman, who is well over sixty years old, is weeping.

When all the speakers have spoken, and participants have asked questions and been answered, the room is cleared, and the people of this city take their hopelessness back to their homes for the night. If they were hoping to gain some relief for their pain at this dialogue, they know now that this was a false hope.

Earlier in the morning, while waiting for the dialogue to begin, a journalist from our paper had told me how he had gone out the night before and witnessed a pair of policemen beating up a woman whom they had stripped down to her underwear. He doesn't know why she was enduring this public beating. He shows me the photos he took on his phone, and I too witness in hazy snapshots the bewilderment of a woman in red panties cowering under a policeman's baton.

One of the last people to leave is Judith Garfield Todd, author of "Through the Darkness" and I sense that she too was weeping. Whether her sorrow is for the past or the present, I do not know. What I do know is that I and thousands of other Zimbabweans want our sorrow to end, want an end to the tears.

***

It is only in recent years that I have come to learn about how childhood trauma affects who we become as adults. It is only in my forties and fifties that I have given myself permission to describe what I witnessed as trauma. Learning how the body keeps score, how the brain rewires around traumatic events helps me attend to myself with compassion. But of course, I cannot help but think of those who do not have the tools at my disposal, who have suffered differently and worse than I have.

I am not as I would have been, had I not survived a genocide in my childhood. Of this I am clear. I know I did not bear the worst of it, because all around, children like me were witnessing greater terrors and suffering worse traumas. All around me, adults are still broken and bearing the physical and psychological scars of that tribal war.

But it is only my own story that I can fully know, only my own salty fear that I can taste.

HERSELF

"Schoolbag in hand, she leaves home in the early morning
Waving goodbye with an absent-minded smile.
I watch her go with a surge of that well-known sadness
And I have to sit down for a while...
Slipping through my fingers all the time
I try to capture every minute
The feeling in it
Slipping through my fingers all the time..."

I play her this song from ABBA and tell her that for me, the song is always about her – that she seems to have been slipping through my fingers from birth. She barely raises an eyebrow. In that peculiarly dismissive, impenetrable phase of fifteen, it is important for her to communicate how little I matter in her life. I don't tell her that when I sing this song about her, I substitute smile with scowl – it is my own private joke to get me through these moments.

The season doesn't last long though. Within months we are almost friends; she is almost smiling when I see her off at the gate, greeting me voluntarily and initiating conversation when I pick her up – a small miracle and I am over the moon. She loves me, and it's OK for me to know this now. But the sweetness of these days is tinged with mounting trepidation for me. She will be leaving very soon and I am not ready for her to go. She, of course, is more than ready. She has been ready to go for some time – almost from birth when I think about it.

She was always herself, this tiny girl. Always quite certain about who she was and her place in the world. Her position as the long awaited, and much beloved only sister of a previously only daughter. Doted on by said sister – like a favourite toy that would be beside her for life.

But never imagine that she was in a shadow of any sort. No, this one defied shadows in much the same way she defied rules that did not make sense and anything really that she did not understand (such things were few and far between) or agree with (such things were plentiful).

Her razor sharp intellect combined with the world's most innocent candour to form a force that would be guaranteed to leave you breathless. Not a naughty child as such, but a wilful one for sure... in that "mom I'm just over here spreading jam on the sofa" way. She was not defiant, and in her mind, I genuinely believe, not even naughty, just curious, determined and candid. Because if you think about it fairly, did you ever remember to tell your child not to spread jam on the sofa? And when you questioned her about why she did not do this or that which you'd instructed her to do, she would say, "Well I really just didn't want to, mum." Calm, polite and searingly truthful, she has left me speechless more times than I can count.

She has always been for herself this child; choosing for herself what she would do and when. From before she was born I could imagine her in the womb, feeling her way toward an exit, palms pressed flat against the walls of her cell, eyes not yet knowing they could open, tracing the curve of my belly to find a way out. A little mermaid with an iron will. That was she.

And when born, she shook off the indignity of helplessness like a pup from a pool, expressing her indignation that we would ever question her competencies – she was always five steps ahead of where she really was. Or perhaps where she really was was five steps behind where we located her. Whatever the case, the tone and pace of her life were set by her and no one else. A diminutive, indignant creature with a fortitude that defied her cute face and hypnotic eyes.

Today she is all milk chocolate and wild honey. The eyes still cast a spell and her matte velvet skin begs to be touched over heightened cheekbones. She will not be drowning anyone in saccharine sweetness though. Those she will fell are slain by the deep and callous mystery of her. The candid word in passing that will make them glow like soft embers in the night or shrink and shirk like slugs in salt water. She has never needed many words, just one or two, smartly chosen and carefully placed will do the trick. I pity the men who will fall for her.

She is strong and yet she is tender. Firm thighs rising to meet coiled up kundalini energy. Shoulders at rest, but not sleeping. She is wide awake, this one. Awake in wit and presence both. As woke as the dark dark eyes in a pool of milky white innocence framed with long long lashes. I am bewitched, I tell you. Breathless.

But when she is in pain. When her heart and her strong self are locked up tight and she will not let us reach her. When heartbreak threatens to bring the solid certainty of her down. When all that is tender about her envelops her like a soft downy blanket which she cannot afford to have anyone touch, lest we cause her damage with our clumsy words and gestures, our awkward attempts to soothe. When that happens, I want to whisper, "Don't go, tiny girl. Don't disappear into yourself. The world needs you tiny tot. Don't go." Because she is so needed. Needed for all the gifts that she brings to the world. Needed to lead.

The world needs her. I need her.

When I look, I see her. I see me. A me I might have been if I were more brave, more beautiful, more clever – just… more.

But if I am honest with myself, I see a me I could never hope to be; not in one hundred million billion years.

HARARE, CIRCA 2007

Today I am counting my blessings. Partly as an antidote to the wave of depression that threatens to overwhelm me, and partly because I really am grateful for the many ways in which I am blessed.

I am thankful for my little family – the four people I now live for and would die for (are you impressed that I included myself? All those hours of therapy must be doing something for my self-esteem!). I am thankful for each individual member – for the tiny baby, still brand new and in perfect health; for her big sister, adjusting to her new role at four years old even as she herself longs to be babied, and for my gentle Christian husband, who has outdone himself in this season as loving attentive spouse, friend, provider, protector and partner.

Today I am thankful that I am in that small group of people who can afford some of the (now) luxuries that make life bearable in Zimbabwe: a car with petrol in the tank, a generator, a water tank, a borehole, a gas cylinder, a freezer full of meat and a well-stocked pantry. These are things I would have taken for granted a year, even a month ago, but today... how suddenly life can change here.

I am thankful even though I will spend the day sitting in bed with my week-old baby because this is the only way I can keep her warm right now. I am thankful even though

Tuesdays and Thursdays are our only two days of definite power supply and today is Tuesday and we have NO power. I am thankful because soon it will be summer, my baby will be older, and the heating problem will matter less.

Yesterday I had an epiphany. I was in the process of changing a very poo-filled nappy when the baby started to produce more poo. It overflowed the nappy, went onto her clothes, onto the bed and finally on the carpet. I could feel the stress levels rising – and then a thought: This is all I have to do today. I don't have to go anywhere, be anyone, or accomplish anything other than taking care of this tiny child. This is all life is asking of me today – I can do this. I felt tremendous peace. I am thankful that I don't have to write a proposal, balance a budget, make a presentation or attend a meeting. I know there are women all over the world who do all this as well as take care of babies – I've been one of them. But this is not what life demands of me in this season, and I am thankful.

In the midst of all this thankfulness, I can't help but be a little angry. And of course, with the anger comes the guilt – every conscious woman's staple food at some point.

I am angry because even though I have a washing machine, I cannot use it because some small pipe is missing and can't be sourced in this city. Even though I have a pantry full of flour, I can't bake a thing because the element for my oven cannot be replaced. I am lucky to have a water tank and a borehole, but they are of no use to me without electricity. I have a gas heater, but I dare not use it "unnecessarily" because we may not be able to replace the gas. Ditto the generator with diesel.

Is this turning into a complaints session? No, it mustn't because I set out to count my blessings. Did I remember to count my family twice?

I am thankful to have you to write to, to think of, to miss. When we think of friends and relatives in the diaspora, it is often with a mixture of envy and anger. We think of lives with a reliable transport system, a predictable power supply and a government that can be trusted as lives of total luxury. When it is time to bury our parents, we resent having to wait for the very important people from overseas to come, while we minions serve the relatives, deal with the inefficiencies of government offices, and manage the family politics. But the truth is, we need you to be out there, we need the money you send to the parents, and the clothes you bring for our kids. And you need us too – to give you roots and assuage your guilt for leaving the folks at their most helpless. So yeah, I'm thankful.

And I miss you.

*P.S: Did you hear the WHO did some research which revealed that 40% of Zimbabwe's population is suffering from mental illness. Are we surprised?

GUESS WHAT?

I drove past your old house today. It looked… *sigh*. Well, it just looked derelict, as if no one lives there. But I know the new people are there because their car was in the garage. But, I mean, other than that, you really would think no one lived there… It's in a sorry state.

I know you said it wasn't Africans, but I just can't help thinking, with the way they're not looking after the place, they must be foreigners or something… or maybe Chinese? There's so many of those around these days.

Anyway, I also saw the talking lady. Remember her? The one who was always talking non-stop while she walked her funny looking dog. She's still all bouncy, lighting up the street as she trots around after her little dog, looking like she doesn't have a care in the world. And yep, still talking to herself as she goes along. Funny old thing.

Guess what? Boy Blue is back. He ran past my house this morning around 6:30. And yes, he's still wearing his blue kit! Can you believe it? I can never tell if it's the same kit he wears or just different clothes in the same shades of blue – he goes by so fast, head down, earphones plugged in, arms pummeling furiously as he scales the hill, looking like a real high-powered running machine. But there's more: I know where he runs to now. And it's not where you think!

Do you remember the route we used to walk in the evenings? Up behind the clusters and then across the golf course? Well, this is where I thought he was running, right? A big 4 km loop and then back home. Well, he doesn't.

Turns out he is running into the clusters, not round them. Running into Number 39 to be exact. Do you know who lives at Number 39 babe? I don't either, but the chick looks Indianish. Maybe Portugese... you just never know with these types? Anyway, he's in there for like half an hour, and then back home he goes to his two toddlers and his wife. What do you think is going on there? An early morning aerobics class? Hahaha is all I can say.

Remember the lady at Number 272, the Matebele chick with the wild Afro? Yeah, she's still at it. I promise you, the number of wine bottles by her bin on Saturday mornings is shocking. You never hear any noise though, so she's not having parties. Just chugging away at the Nederburgs and Namaquas, with the occasional splurge on a Rupert and Rothschild. And then two days after the wine bottles, the washing line is literally covered in lace and chiffon!

What do you think she really does in there? I only ever see her when she puts her laundry out. I mean, some of that stuff is barely there at all. It's like outlines of nighties and g-strings, teddies – no man, not the cuddly kind, the type you wear – and silky dressing gowns that dry in minutes. I mean, if I wasn't so meticulous about keeping an eye out, I would miss half of it. What? Well, that's how flimsy the fabric is. No sooner has she hung it up to dry than it's ready to collect.

The other day she did a load that was all black. You should have seen it, hun. There were fishnet stockings – when was the last time you saw anyone in fishnets! Well, yes Beyonce does wear them all the time, but hers aren't black. Anyway, there was everything you could think of: camisoles, bras, and French knickers even! She even had something with feathers, though I'm not quite sure what it was. I don't even know why she washed it. But, wow, man. It was quite a collection.

I never get to see her visitors, so I just can't figure out what all that fancy shit is for. I mean, if she has a gentleman caller then he must be the world's most discreet person. I don't see him arrive, and I never see him go. And you know from our position on the hill we see everything that goes on in those clusters. Someone said something about CIO guys but I immediately changed the subject coz you just never know who's who around here, and the walls have ears. But just imagine if it's true…giiiirrrrrl!

Speaking of who's who, I nearly walked straight past that bird with the big car at the supermarket yesterday. Didn't recognise her from a bar of soap with her new hairstyle. Guess what? It's red! Not red like a redhead, but like bright brilliant red – pillar box red, Coca-cola red. It's karayzieeee! Honestly, I don't know how these girls keep changing their hair like that. It must cost a fortune. And I believe some of those styles take hours and hours to do. Imagine spending a whole day on your hair when you could be playing a game of golf or something. Ha! That could never be me.

I miss you man. This neighbourhood is changing all the time and I just don't know how we're going to stop everything from going down the drain like the rest of the country. Maybe I should have left when you guys went, but I just couldn't let all my investments here go to waste. You were right to keep most of your money outside – it's my outside funds that I'm living on now. These people have really ruined everything. Now I hear they're passing some kind of law to take a percentage of our businesses – some kind of indigenisation act or something. Can you imagine doll! If that happens, I'm out. I'm not sticking around to live through another round of what they did on the farms.

The crazy thing is, they can't see it. Can't see how they're destroying everything. Ah well. God knows what will happen when all the good people are gone. They'll be left to fend for themselves.

HEN PARTY

"Ha! But your friend though," the two girls at the sink made eye contact and laughed simultaneously. "That was a bit desperate sis, *eish*. I mean, yes you have to fight for your man, but where is our pride?"

"Yah, desperation can make you do wild things," said Patience, pulling a face before adding, "Shame."

"But we're all desperate." Chiedza said quietly. "In our own ways, we're all wilding."

This kind of truth was not welcome at what was supposed to be a festive hen party, and Patience instantly wished she had followed her initial instinct to leave Chiedza off the guest list. But the party was too small as it was, and though she had labelled it intimate and tried to sell it to herself and others as a cosy affair that should be the envy of all those not invited, in her heart of hearts she knew this was not true. She had only invited five people to Eva's party because those were the only people she knew who genuinely wished Eva well on her second attempt at marriage. It was in direct contrast to Eva's first one which was held at a hotel because of the large number of guests. The plush decor and sumptuous buffet heralded a life of affluence awaiting the happy bride, who was doing her best – unsuccessfully for the most part – not to seem too smug.

But in spite of the promises held in that first party, the rounds of auntly advice and saucy bedroom games played, and oh, the gifts – the fine crockery and silverware, the appliances and linens – in spite of it all, Eva never got to take that longed-for walk down the aisle, nor did she secure the promised happily ever after to follow. Her groom had failed to show up for the *lobola* ceremony, which had been postponed twice already due to unexpected business related travel on his part. The postponements were how the party had ended up being held before lobola was paid. Those who had muttered that it was bad form had been accused of jealousy, and so had shut their mouths until the groom had proven his fickleness, at which point they released their I-told-you-sos into the community with heads held high and smiles of triumph.

The five friends gathered here today were an odd assortment. There was chubby Hazel, from the HR department of the estate agency where Eva worked. Slightly older than the other girls, with a warm calming aura, Hazel and Eva had bonded over the personal crises in their respective lives. Hazel suffering the heartache of multiple miscarriages, and Eva burning with the shame of her failed-before-it-started "marriage". There was Anesu, posh and poised, who was kind of related to Eva, but not closely enough to be influenced by the army of relatives that was against the upcoming union. And then there was bubbly Thandie, round-faced with matching spherical breasts like grapefruits and a high backside that jiggled playfully, in sync with her animated yellow face. Thandie was more Patience's friend really, but had borne witness to the growing friendship between Patience and her neighbour, Eva, which had landed them here today. She'd been invited on account of her irrepressible good humour, her encyclopaedic knowledge of sex, which came from her vast exploration of all things sexual, and her tendency to veer towards the lurid. Basically, she was the one-man hype squad whose job tonight was to keep things saucy and fun. Then of course there was killjoy Chiedza, effectively the opposite of Thandie, she was a tall, slim, quiet girl who hardly ever smiled and was Eva's childhood friend.

Patience's apartment was small by any standard, identical to the one Eva occupied next door. The flats were designed for single people, but further down the corridor, Patience knew there were young couples with one or two children, and downstairs there were more young families living in what must be pretty cramped conditions. Nevertheless, the buildings were well maintained and the block was secure, with a carport for each flat, which is what the main attraction had been for Patience.

She couldn't believe Eva had committed herself to becoming one half of one of those couples, starting their marriage in a bachelor pad. They had talked so differently in their evening chats when they had visited each other to eat together or watch movies or when they had shopped together for groceries and clothes and household furniture. Why did Eva's dreams suddenly plummet like that? Had she just been playing along to keep Patience company? It was impossible to tell.

Patience knew that a big part of Eva's struggle was overcoming the trauma that Munya had caused when he pretended he was going to marry her. He had embarrassed Eva and left her to carry the burden of shame with her family, friends, church and community. It was really awful, and Patience's heart went out to her. But it wasn't like she was pregnant or anything. And Munya, who had been loaded, didn't leave her with any debt or financial scandal – Patience felt Eva could be grateful for that at least. Now she was with Ignatius, who could barely feed himself, let alone look after a wife and family.

Up until Eva revealed, in a moment of weakness, that she had lent Ignatius the money to pay for her *lobola*, Patience had not realised how wretched her situation was and had been unable to disguise the horror on her face. Eva quickly tried to make light of it. "It's a loan, friend. His commission didn't come in when he thought it would." Patience hadn't argued, but she'd gone back to her place that night feeling sad. It wasn't like Eva *needed* to get married – she just wanted to cover over the awkwardness of her previous disaster. She wanted to stick it to the world by acquiring a status that said, "See, I'm not the one who had a problem. It was him. I'm happily married now. Someone wants me." Patience could see how being deserted at the altar, which is basically what had happened, could leave a girl with serious abandonment issues. Eva's own father had left for the UK when she was in primary school and never returned, so the fiasco with Munya was probably underlining an existing rejection complex.

She sighed as she looked around the room at the girls gathered for Eva's second send off.

She knew Eva was desperate, but was Chiedza right in saying they all were? Was there a whole generation of young women wilding in desperation, and if so, what were they desperate for or about? Where was their desperation coming from?

Hazel was concentrating on arranging snacks on a platter, her dark lips pursed in concentration. There wasn't much time before Eva would arrive, and they had all come to the party from work. They were going to surprise her on arrival, pop some Prosecco and snacks before watching a short video that Thandie had brought. Patience hadn't seen it, and she hoped that it wouldn't be too gruesome for the other girls. She herself didn't mind watching dirty movies, and there'd been many times in the past where she and Thandie had started to experiment after watching some girl on girl action. She wasn't sure how the others felt though, and doubted whether the likes of Chiedza and Anesu had much of a clue about what was possible in bed.

As if on cue, Anesu's dulcet tones broke through Patience's reverie, "You're right Chichi," Anesu was the kind of posh that loved pet names and diminutives, "Everybody's wilding in their own way. My cousin just came out of Revival House after a month and went straight back to her boyfriend's place. They partied till three in the morning." Revival House was the rehab facility where the rich and reckless took their errant kids when they didn't know what else to do with them. All the girls chimed in with expressions of shock and sympathy. "The parents have completely lost control of that girl. Ever since she had a miscarriage…"

It was like watching shutters come down over Hazel's face. She didn't need to imagine the desperation in Anesu's cousin because she had been through the same situation four times. Her husband's people were starting to murmur. What exactly the murmurs were saying, Hazel did not know, but her pain was palpable. Her husband had been supportive and strong at first. But now, he too seemed to fault her somehow, to imply with his distant silence that this was her fault. With the last one she hadn't even told him she was pregnant, and when she lost the baby, she would have bled to death alone at home if her helper hadn't happened to come into the main house just then. Her road was a lonely one, and she couldn't see who could help her, or how. She needed to fix her marriage, and the only way to do it was with a baby.

Patience worried about the sombre tone in the room. She urgently needed this gathering to turn into a party and wondered what had happened to Thandie, the failsafe party maker. "Who's got the playlist girls?" She was hoping the interruption would shift the energy in the room. "Where's Thandi?" The others looked around. Thandi was nowhere to be seen.

Anesu offered to pull up her Spotify list, but no one imagined she would have the kind of music the occasion needed. Her tastes tended toward international trends rather than local ones. Patience doubted if she knew even one local artist by name. "Let me find Thandi," she said.

It didn't take long to go through the rooms in the flat and Patience decided to check for Thandie in the corridor outside in case she had gone out to make a call. She wasn't prepared for what she saw.

There was Thandie, lips locked in a lingering kiss with Ignatius right outside her door. She shook her head to clear her vision because surely, she could not be seeing right. "Thandie! What the hell *sisi*..." Slowly, reluctantly, Thandie pulled away. Then, seeing Patience's horrified face, Ignatius made a beeline for the fire escape. He wasn't going to be answering any questions from his fiancee's friend tonight.

"But Thandie..." Patience began.

"Oh relax *mukoma kani*. It's not like we're dating..." she giggled. "I'm just helping a brother get a bit of a budget bachelors' party before Eva signs him out of the dating pool for good. It's called *umjolo* sis. Nothing serious. In fact, in this case, you could call it community service."

Patience couldn't contain the confusion in her head, so she decided to leave the matter alone. Thandie followed her

59

inside and got stuck in bringing music, energy and her signature party vibe to the evening.

By the time Eva arrived, the girls were halfway through a second bottle of wine. It was starting to feel like a party, and even Anesu's accent was starting to lose its hyper-nasal twang. The incident in the corridor was all but forgotten, and Eva seemed genuinely surprised and pleased by her friends' effort to give her a send off.

"Ok my people," declared Thandie an hour later, when Hazel's delicious snacks had been polished and everyone was starting to act tipsy, "time to give our bride-to-be some advice before we watch the movie, which let me assure you is XXX rated." As she said this, Thandie bent down and stuck her bottom up in the air, waving it in their faces like a pair of balloons. There were shrieks of laughter and fake outrage as the girls got an eyeful of her red bikini exposed by her super short mini skirt.

Everyone except Chiedza was eager to see and hear more. "This is not your auntie's kitchen tea Thandie. Can't we skip the advice."

"Nope," said Thandie, pretending to be serious. "That's the most important aspect of the evening. We have to equip our girl Eva to succeed in her position as Mai Kabasa." Through the murmurs of protest, the girls agreed to give a one-line piece of advice each. "I'll go last," said Thandie, putting herself in charge as usual. "Chiedza can start."

Fuelled with wine, song and laughter, Patience giggled to herself. *I see what you did there, Thandie*, she thought to herself. *We are going from the worst to the best.*

"Once you've made your bed, you have to lie in it," said Chiedza when there was a lull in the noise. "That's it. That's my one-line advice." No one was surprised by her sanctimonious offering.

It was Hazel's turn next. "Watch out for those wicked in-laws."

Well, that's not particularly useful, thought Patience. *What exactly is Eva supposed to do with that?* But she could see that Hazel was advising from her own position of pain, and there was really nothing anyone could do about it.

Anesu said, "Always keep a little something for yourself – a little money, a little time, a little power." Everyone was so surprised by this wisdom coming from Anesu, they all turned to look at her.

"Wow," said Eva. "I'll try to remember that."

Patience didn't know what to tell her friend. She thought about Eva's journey, her valiant attempts at fixing her life, the incident she herself had witnessed between Thandie and Ignatius earlier. Eventually she blurted out, "Nothing matters as much as you think it does. Only you matter. You're the one you have to live with all your life, so take care of you first."

No one complained that Patience's advice was more than one line. The room fell silent.

"Well," Thandie said, breaking the serious mood, "My advice is, make sure you always have a girlfriend available to take out your frustrations on."

"What?" Cried Patience for the second time that night. She was joined by a chorus of protests from the other girls. "Thandie are you actually crazy?"

Suddenly the TV screen flickered on as Thandie started running the movie. "Relax girls, you'll understand what I mean in a minute." As the opening sequence brought up the movie title, *Water Lilies*, together with footage of two busty girls in bikinis fondling one another, everybody burst into laughter.

CARDS

He sat across the table from her, looking small because he wore clothes that were slightly too big for him. *Why do men do that*, she thought absent-mindedly. Perhaps he thinks it will make him look bigger. She struggled to contain her smirk at the idea of such foolishness. Like women who thought wearing clothes that were too small would make them look slimmer, she thought. These were problems unfamiliar to Vimbayi whose perfect frame meant that clothes generally fit like they were tailored specifically for her.

She hadn't expected the awkwardness around the exchange, the silences between the pleasantries. She had long since learnt not to rush to fill silences. "Why make it my responsibility?" she had decided several years ago. After all, silence can be a powerful weapon. She tried to relax and leave it to him to slay the silence. He struggled. Moving the conversation along to the business of the day, she deftly rescued him and thought with a sigh, *I hope this is not how it will be when we are together - me continually rescuing him.*

Up until that point, she had taken the fact that they would sleep together as a foregone conclusion. She never considered that he might not warm to her charms because she had made up her mind it was time for things in her life to change, and there he was.

In the months that followed, the thing she would remember most about that first meeting was the exchange of business cards. When her mind ran over the incident, this part always played out in slow motion; how he drew out his wallet while he was speaking, pulled out the card and lay it on the table, ensuring it was the right way up for her to read the contents before sliding it across the table towards her. She in turn swivelled in her big chair to pick a card out of the Perspex box that sat behind her desk, placed it on the table and slid it toward him.

Sales Representative, flashed his title on the tiny piece of red card which threatened to ruin everything, and Chief Executive Officer, responded hers on its whisper grey background. In the movie of her memory, this moment was always played out as an overhead shot, with the aerial view of them sitting across the table from one another and their respective business cards traversing the expanse of the table between them in opposite directions like ships passing in the night.

Ships passing in the night. This was what their marriage had become. After the excitement of being unequally yoked, the drama of family squabbles, the triumph of defying convention and church and all things sensible, they were married. Beyond those first heady days, they soon settled into a monotony that she couldn't have imagined. Could life really be so dry, so dusty, like objects on display that were never moved? Could living with someone she had chosen, handpicked herself in fact, be so joyless? How was this her life?

Within a year she had stopped asking herself these questions. She blamed television and the entertainment industry at large for fuelling her fantasies about how married life could be. She knew now that companionship, intimacy and joy were rarities of relationships, not the norm.

At first, she had worked on his image, trading his oversized suits in for slicker cuts. His shoes with the curling up toes disappeared as she replaced them with improved versions in black and dark brown only. She was careful to present these changes as gifts because she had heard that men resented it when women tried to change them. Soon he was a modern, streamlined version of his former self – like a cellphone upgrade. On weekends he wore linen shirts with his slim fit jeans rather than baggy tracksuits, and in the office, everyone started to address him as if he was more senior and more successful than his peers until he became exactly that.

When his business card changed from red to navy, signifying his ascension from staff to management, she breathed a sigh of relief. Surely this closing of the income and status gap between them would now help them become closer at home. They could have similar friend groups and start to feel like a proper couple with couple friends.

What she hadn't reckoned was that her own trajectory would change too. She became president of the association of

Actuarial Scientists in the region, a highly prestigious position with innumerable benefits. She travelled more, interacted with a wider circle of ever more powerful people, negotiated bigger deals and was often pushed forward as the representation of women who were "making it" in the industry.

He was loyal to a fault. Kept his circle of friends that he'd had since his days at the polytechnic. He refused to drive his big new SUV – another "gift" from her – when he went to play boozers soccer with them on Friday nights or when he visited his relatives in the townships on Sundays. He confounded her by holding tightly to his world, a world whose benefits she simply couldn't comprehend.

And these were the petitions she brought to her God on Sunday mornings when she made her weekly pilgrimage to the glamorous Pentecostal church down the road from their luxury northern suburbs home. At first, she asked God to change him, to fill him with more ambition, to open his eyes to the treasures and joys she saw, to make him want what she wanted. Later she thought maybe that was not quite right and began asking God to help her understand him better. If anything, she understood him less with every passing year. Eventually she stopped talking to God altogether and made peace with the fact that going to church was just one more thing she did to expand her network, improve her social life and maintain her image.

In the movie of her life, the overhead camera was no longer giving ceiling shots, but rather outdoor drone-style footage, taken from high in the sky. It showed a lonely highway, and a luxury car driving northwards, to a neighbourhood where the roads were lined with blooming jacarandas. It passed a small hatchback, driving the opposite direction, toward a shanty town where every vehicle took chances creating its own road. The camera changed angles slightly to show the drivers of both cars - a woman in one, a man in the other, each one alone.

PACKING

Barbara was packing and unpacking. Repacking her things. A neat freak, they had called her years ago. She never liked it when her things were awry… spilling over or otherwise not in order. She wanted things to sit where they were meant to be, a place for everything and everything in its place, not wild and out of control like some undisciplined toddler.

It had been too long she realised, since she'd done a proper clean up. Some of the things had dried on, creating impossible stains; others morphed to become a part of their containers. With the passage of time and the lack of disturbance, some had grown roots and committed to staying. It would be a lot. She would need some tools: a notebook, music, a pen, a pillow, a box of tissues, no, make that a roll. This was heavy duty after all. And so it began.

She thought about starting at the beginning. At the place in Mpopoma where she had been born, where she had learnt that she was different, where she had seen that a blessing can be a curse, where she had discovered a 'them' and an 'us'. But that stuff was too far down the bottom of the box, and she couldn't reach it without first attending to the stuff closer to the top.

Starting at the top would be easiest, she supposed, but all the stuff at the top was still fresh, still pulsating in front of her threateningly, still too real. Just thinking about it made her feel like there was a weight bearing down on her chest. Thinking about the betrayal made her shoulders stiffen, her throat close and her breath become shallow. The betrayal stuff was hard, and it was also complicated. It had one long tap root which was her sister, and a couple of offshoots of that, like the people she'd thought were her friends, and the man she'd thought she would marry. Above the ground, out in the sunshine there was so much more. The betrayal had branches that stretched wide across the sky of her life, blocking out the sun. It was leafy with long needle-sharp thorns. How did one begin to trim and tidy something like this? Like a weed that starts out pesky but harmless, and ends up a whole tree, a forest even. It was a large, ugly thorn bush growing right out of her heart, dropping its leaves and its needles everywhere, making a prickly, painful mess.

There was her mother, "I warned you to stay away from that fool!" Barbara had looked up at her mother's bulging eyes and the mouth blooming like a giant teapot spout. "I said it wouldn't end well, didn't I? Yes! I said it."

Asked and answered, thought Barbara.

"Now look, what a disaster!" her mother had waved her hand towards the table she was standing over as if to indicate the actual spot where the mess might be located.

Barbara sighed.

There had been nothing to see on that worn out pink Formica table. Nothing that most people would be able to see anyway. If you were a seasoned member of the family though, like Barbara was, you might have been able to see years' worth of shame, decades of recrimination and multiple collections of I-told-you-sos sitting in jagged piles on that table. If you were a member of the family and you ran your hand over that smooth pale plastic that had been so fashionable in the seventies when the table was purchased, you would feel the invisible scars left by decades of wounded leadership.

This table was where her mother had delivered her many lifesaving sermons over the years, sermons designed to threaten her offspring into lives of piety and grace or alternatively, to assure them of the murky future that awaited them if they did not heed her counsel. Barbara wanted to believe it was those sermons that drove her sister down her chosen path of least resistance and into the bowels of the great betrayal. She needed to believe that for everything to make sense. But she'd been subject to the same sermons, and here she was, a victim. What she didn't understand was why, as the one who had been betrayed, she was also the one who got to carry the shame.

At this table was where Barbara now laid out her tools. She wondered if what she had brought would be sufficient for this job. It was starting to seem like it might need something more drastic: a blade perhaps, some antiseptic ointment and good bandages, the kind from the pharmacy, not the supermarket. It had been years since she had invoked this particular ritual of tidying in her life. But she remembered the relief, oh my! Once the blade had cut through the skin, once the blood had bulged gently through the slit and was flowing, it made her understand why the expression "bloodletting" existed; once the initial pain was felt, the relief was marvellous. Yes, marvellous was the right word because she marvelled at how effective it was.

Everything that lay heavy on her soul became light again. And when it wasn't effective, she just made a few more cuts, a little harder, a little deeper, and it was sublime. The first time she had done it she immediately understood why hard drugs were so addictive. That instant relief was like nothing else on earth. She was always careful to cut high enough up her arm that she could hide the wound properly. She could wear long sleeved shirts with her pencil skirts and soaring heels and no one would be any the wiser. She would still be the cool, competent executive that her subordinates knew and admired. When it got hot, she could roll up her sleeves and still no one would know her secret; no one would wonder why she never went sleeveless. Nothing to see here.

But that was years ago, and she was older now. All those therapy sessions must surely have counted for something – for better tools, and less of a bloody mess, for healthier choices? She skipped the top layer and reached down to what lay beneath it, just under the top. Seemed like it wasn't easiest to start at the top after all. Beneath the betrayal she found a tangled collection of threads. Some were strong and ropy, others brightly coloured, silken and fragile. They crisscrossed each other, forming loops and knots and in some places, she could see there was no way to loosen and untangle without simply cutting some of those threads free. She started with the delicate ones, ones that could twist and snap at the slightest application of pressure. She wanted to try and preserve them intact – the tentative pride in her achievements, the bit she got to enjoy quietly at home in the bath. It was bright and blue and beautiful. She wondered how it had come to be tied up in so many knots. Something so lovely now sullied by all the garbage surrounding it.

She thought about her big mistake. At least, that was the euphemism her mother used to refer to the error of judgement that had almost cost Barbara her life. It was her first semester at college, that first taste of freedom. She had been in love, and he had promised her... well. It didn't matter now. How big and how bitter was the pill of humility she had swallowed when it all came tumbling down. It almost choked her as she forced it down her throat with apologies she did not mean, and deference to people she did not respect. What a season that had been.

She picked up her pen and wrote to the child she would never birth, remembering it all.

You too would have learnt to say you are sorry with a hardened heart and frozen eyes," she wrote furiously. *You will say sorry like it is a curse that you are spitting at someone, with a ball of tightly rolled phlegm and frustration, at a velocity you cannot measure or imagine. You will say sorry and the word will be a weapon, designed and directed specifically to cause harm. Nonetheless the apology box will be ticked, and inside you, there will be a perverse pleasure in knowing that the recipient of your apology is in no way fooled by the word but has to accept it because it was she who drew the box and required you to tick it. And what really can they say after you have apologised? If they accuse you of not meaning it, they will seem petty and churlish. They will accept your apology in silence. You will win. Even though it will feel like losing, you will have won.*

She reached further down and pulled out the dusty layers of her career. Just looking at the journey and the milestones made her jaw tighten. She forced herself to breathe – one long breath in and then out again. It had been eleven years now, and still she could not seem to earn the respect she knew she deserved. At first, she had tried really hard, doing grunt work, picking up balls that everyone else dropped, volunteering for extra assignments. But no extra rewards came her way apart from verbal accolades. There was always a surplus of those. But money, power, position? Forget about that!

She moved jobs and realised the problem hadn't been with her employer. The problem was in the system. Even when she got the better positions with powerful titles, they still expected her to serve tea in the Executive Committee meetings. She still earned less than idiotic Givemore who didn't even have a postgraduate qualification but was supposed to be her counterpart. In spite of the admiration of the youngsters, she faced a lot of humiliation behind the boardroom door. Her lips pursed as she thought about it: the verbal jabs thrown her way; the inside jokes shared by the mostly male team in her presence were bad enough, but the outside jokes about women and hormones were so much worse. And she had known any reaction from her would just be more "proof" that they were right, that women were oversensitive and difficult. So she remained silent and swallowed her anger. Swallowed it over and over and over again for years, until she was full of it. Until the simmering pot of angry porridge inside her reached a temperature that was in danger of boiling over. Until it made her gasp. Until it consumed her, even as she moved to seemingly better jobs, and better positions, with yet more adoring direct reports and better perks. The bigger the car she drove, the more the gossiping voices rose – once or twice they had even made it into the press, casting aspersions on her abilities, questioning her capacity and laying to waste her thousands of hours of study, of experience, of service. Her face was a tight ball of fury now. The nylon ropes of tension pulled taught across it, binding it with lines that marred her beauty and captured her chest.

"I have to let it go," she whispered to herself. She knew this was true, because otherwise the tidying up exercise would be futile. Well, not completely futile, but it would not be the resounding success she had hoped for. If she was honest with herself, she had to admit that it was never really a resounding success.

It was always this way with the anger. Her tools could scrape away almost all of the debris in her life, but the anger remained, a stubborn stain that always left a shadow, no matter how much she cleaned. The only other thing more resilient than the anger was the fear. The Fear.

That's what sat at the very bottom of the pile. That's what kept all the other stinky things alive and well fed, and gave them a solid, immovable foundation. She had no tool for it. No breathing exercise that could suppress it. No mindfulness instrument that tamed it. And now that she had disturbed all the other contents of her bursting at the seams box, now that she had shattered the tenuous peace in the hive, The Fear arose.

Beneath the incomplete letter to her unborn child she wrote 'The Fear'. She capitalised the words to signify its significance in her life, its importance and how it featured in every decision she had ever made. She thought about all the desperate things she had done. The desperate choices she had made, born of a need for redemption, or restitution. Born of a fear of failing, fear of falling apart, fear of not becoming who she was expected to be and subsequently being rejected, fear of everyone knowing that she wasn't in fact who she purported to be. The Fear was all consuming and overwhelming.

Barbara looked up from the table at the fluorescent light above her. She'd wanted to finish this process before her mother came home. But since she had poked the bear that The Fear was, she now sat paralysed. She was choking on The Fear and although she swallowed and swallowed, she could not dispel it. In fact, it left her with an after taste of anger. There was only one way to make it all go away. Only one thing left to do, to tidy up her life once and for all. She would make the mess go away forever.

While the bath water was running, she rummaged at the back of the bathroom cupboard and found her tools. There was an unopened pack of razor blades, some antiseptic ointment and well, there would be no need for bandages this time. If she did the job right, there would be no need for much of anything ever again.

MISUNDERSTOOD

Baby,

The chasm that has grown between us isn't really one about money. I think we both know this. It isn't even about disclosures of any description. It is about the distance that grows between two people when they stop sharing themselves. It is about intimacy and the things that make a marriage genuine, honest and real.

The thing is, I want intimacy with my wife. I want us to be able to be vulnerable with one another, without fear. I know this will be difficult because so much has passed between us. It will be difficult because I have hurt you in the past, because I have not always been transparent, because I have not always listened to you or given you my trust. I know it will be hard for you to take the chance to trust me again, but I am asking you to do it, so that we can both begin to heal.

I want you to know that I am ready. I am ready to leave my ego, my preconceived notions, my mistrust and my pain at the door; and enter into a new conversation with you. I am willing to pay the price because I believe the intimacy we regain will be worth more than that.

I need to know if you want this too? I am inviting you to believe in the marriage we once believed we could have – a real partnership. I am inviting you to lay down your weapons and your armour at the same door that I am leaving mine, to start a new conversation. It will be scary I know, but it's worth the risk.

Please understand that I too am afraid. I am afraid of reaching out and finding that you reject me. I am afraid of us trying and failing and what that will mean for our marriage going forward. I am afraid of showing you all of me and finding that you only show me a portion of you. I am afraid to be vulnerable after so many years of keeping my guard up.

What frightens me the most about us is the feeling that I am in a marriage, not with a woman, but with a whole collection of people. That there is no me and you (singular) but rather me and you (plural). I understand that family is important to you, but I want your first family to be with me. I want to be your next of kin the way we imagined it would be the day we married. I want to know that whatever you and I plan or discuss is about you and I until we're BOTH ready to share, until we've agreed that we're ready to share.

But of course, you need a reason to give up the comfort of what is familiar, the joy of sharing everything with people you trust and feel secure with. I realise I am not those people right now, and that hurts. But I'm willing to take responsibility for failing to ensure that I would be, and I hope you can come to trust me all the same. Here's why:

1. I am for you. I am, first and foremost, for us. For the partnership we have built. If I haven't demonstrated this in

the past, I give you my assurance that I will do so from today. I am for you. I am for us.

2. I will cover you. Again, I understand if you have difficulty believing this because in the past I have left you exposed, vulnerable, lonely. It was remiss of me, and I have no one to blame but myself for you having to find another source of comfort and cover. This won't happen anymore.

3. I get you. I get that you are afraid. That you are angry at the way in which I have failed you in the past. I get that you have watched me build walls around myself instead of bridges. That I have shut you out instead of drawing you in. That I have not demonstrated leadership in raising and resolving the issues that lie between us. That ends today. If you will have me, I want to take my rightful place as the head of our house once more, not to dominate and direct you, but to demonstrate the kind of love that God has for his people

I have laid bare what is in my heart, and how I hope to serve you, as a husband and a life partner. But I am only one part of a pair. We can't repair the unit by only repairing me.

I need to know if you too are willing to reach out, to be vulnerable, to share your hurts and your fears. To make me your next of kin, and the head of our home. I can't fix this by myself. I need you.

***

Honey,

You said just the things I hoped you would say. It's like you unlocked the door to my inner diary and read every entry and answered it. Any woman who could read your letter would wonder why her husband can't articulate himself like this, why he can't commit the way you do. How can I say anything after all you've said? There is nothing to dispute, nothing to disagree with. And for me, in many ways, that's a big part of the problem. Let me explain.

Your words have never been a problem, never been in short supply, never fallen foul of even the highest international standards of romance. Your declarations are as epic as your marriage proposal was to me – on a boat, with an audience of hundreds, everyone dressed in white, do you remember? You say the things you are supposed to say, and when required, you perform your role as loving husband to perfection.

But you don't love me, Mudiwa. You only perform. You pretend. You present the pictures and the world – me included – buys in. But you don't know how to be real except on paper and in pictures. You don't know how to husband and how to father and you can't know how to do those things because you don't know how to be. Just be. You are like that kid in class that can pass any exam but can never explain a concept to you. You only know how to get the marks.

And so it makes it hard for me to sign up to everything you are suggesting. I feel that I would be signing up for a job from just reading the company vision statement. But strategy *yacho*? *Dololo*! I gravitate towards my family because I know who they are. You on the other hand... you're like our daughter's imaginary friend that she had in pre-school. Do you remember? Perfect, but without substance.

So while I long to close the chasm between us, to bridge the distance that has grown, to mend the places we have torn asunder in our heart, I can't see how that can happen while you remain the way you are. You have made me best supporting actress in the production that is your life, starring yourself, and I am not willing to come out of the wings and continue this charade. Our life cannot be an Instagram story my love.

What I need from you is to be real. What I need is for you to stop with the beautifully crafted words and the whispers, to put pause to the posing and just be real with me. Be that person you are at night in the last minutes of wakefulness, before you fall asleep, when there is no audience, and there is no opportunity for applause. That's the place you will find yourself. And then you will find me.

SATAN & CO

Sabona Satane

She smiled as she typed the text message. These early morning digital trysts were the most delicious part of her day – except when she was going to see him of course – then the whole day just arranged itself cosily around the moment they would finally be together.

Slingo sam... uvukanjani? Ungiphuphile yini?

He had christened her Slingo, meaning temptation, right at the beginning of their affair, and had even saved her number under that name. But that was before his wife got hold of his phone. That first time, she had been all weepy and victimy in that why-would-you-do-this-to-me, what-have-I-ever-done-to-deserve-this way that wives do. He of course apologised, said it was nothing and bought her the new double mirrored door fridge that she had been wanting.

He changed her name in his phone after that, but not before he made sure the number wasn't in his wife's phone. He had become meticulous about closing any loopholes that might get him into trouble again. Not that he minded purchasing big ticket apology items – actually he got a kick out of that – but the admin was too much. The tears, tantrums, weeks of good behaviour, pretending he had changed his ways... It really took the fun out of the game.

The first time Gift had committed adultery was just a few days after the *lobola* ceremony. He had expected to feel guilty, but he didn't. He thought perhaps after the white wedding, when he'd actually made vows about faithfulness and forsaking all others and all that crap, but even then, he felt fine. Everything was just exactly the same as when he had cheated on girls while he was dating – maybe more exciting because the stakes were higher, but otherwise the same. He had never really had only one girlfriend at a time.

Cynthia was a lot of fun. She understood the rules of the game and she played it well – teasing, taunting one minute and then giving him her all explosive passionate encounters the next, only to disappear again in a heartbeat. After he christened her *Slingo*, she returned fire with a host of names of her own, depending on her mood.

When she was trying to focus on something at work, he was *Mkhohlisi*, a distraction. In times when she pretended to be bored with their relationship – those made him really nervous – he was *Scefe*, an annoyance. When she was deeply satiated with their lovemaking, or provoking him to think about it, he was *Satane*, the devil himself, she said because sin never tasted so good as when she sinned with him.

He couldn't understand how a man could ever get bored with a woman like Cynthia and considered the fellow who had divorced her a fool. With no kids to keep her down and just her job as the Executive Director of an international NGO to consume her attention, he didn't have a lot of competition, and he liked it that way. She travelled a lot and occasionally he was able to synchronise his own invented business trips with hers.

Cynthia hadn't always dated married men. In fact, in her own marriage she had been a faithful and loving wife. Coming from a conservative background, she'd been a virgin when she married and she revelled in the discovery of her own sexuality under the tutelage of her husband, a more worldly older companion. They had been happy for the most part, but when he started pressuring her to have kids and she wasn't ready, their happy union started to wobble.

By the time she learnt that he had made a young girl in his mother's neighbourhood pregnant, they were in a very bad space. Still, she hadn't expected him to go so far left so fast. She found it impossible to reconcile her vision for life with the idea of being one of who-knows-how-many wives.

Learning to navigate life after divorce was the thing that really traumatised her. She made the discovery that life was divided into two worlds, one populated by married women, children and spinsters, the other by men, single moms and divorcees. The second world appeared to be the real world, while the other, she christened Lalaland.

In Lalaland, where she had lived as a young woman and as a wife, everyone took marriage seriously. Everyone thought vows were real and everyone genuinely meant well. At least that's what she understood.

But in the real world, people laughed when you said you wouldn't date someone because they were married. No one cared about anything except money and survival. Oh, and pleasure. People in the real world loved to have a good time, and they didn't let silly concepts like loyalty or fidelity get in the way.

When she entered the real world, she was immediately approached by friends of her ex-husband who wanted to take care of her, buy her gifts, include her in their travel plans and even pay her rent. At first, she was puzzled because their approach didn't seem to take into account their wives, who were her friends after all. She didn't stay puzzled for long though. The game and its rules became apparent quite rapidly and though she resisted valiantly, the pressure was intense and unrelenting.

Then one day, she met Satan. He was sweet. And smart. Instead of leading with offers of material comforts with an unspoken quid pro quo, he positioned himself as a friend. Oh how she needed a confidant in those early days, someone with whom she could untangle the confusion that was her new social status. He had understood when she talked about the two worlds, about not belonging to either of them, about being completely alone even though she was surrounded by community.

Before she knew it, he had helped her cross over from Lalaland to the real world, and after the first few pangs of conscience, it turned out to be an OK place to live. She found that once she got to grips with the rules of the game, she was actually quite good at it, and even if it meant the deadening of her heart, she played to win.

Cynthia turned over in her bed, her arms ploughing through the many pillows that now populated it. Stretching her entire body like a spoilt cat, she found her phone and giggled as she read his reply.

Zwana Satane... she typed. Listen Satan...

It was about to be a good day outside Lalaland.

ASANTE UNBORN

Initially it just wasn't a priority, let's face it. She was in university and then she was a sparkling young graduate with a great future, and then she was job-hunting and making all those really critical early career decisions that can sometimes determine the whole trajectory of your life. That needed a lot of focus. Even her mother agreed, though her father had seemed a bit quiet about it all. She thought perhaps he might have been hoping she would join him in the business, but he'd never said so explicitly, and she wasn't keen anyway. After all, her brother Mazvita was there.

There'd been some great offers from important companies: a global agency offering her an internship in Nigeria, to which mother had categorically said absolutely not. How short-sighted, she'd argued passionately, partly just to annoy her mum and partly because she was young and smart and could build a solid argument for her position. "You can't judge a whole country by the tiny percentage of criminals that you've heard about. And besides, it's the fastest growing economy in Africa right now." Her mother was having none of it.

Then there was the local firm offering her a junior role with a fast track to partnership. It would be a modest start, but it was a safe bet working in a familiar environment with an assured future. And the bonus was that she would get to the top before all her peers, which appealed to her competitive nature. She had eventually settled for a graduate training programme with a multinational bank. Her mother reasoned that the perks would include favourable mortgage terms, allowing her to get onto the property ladder early in life so as to secure her personal wealth before marriage.

What she hadn't told her mother was that the programme included an overseas placement in the second year, and she was eager to work in the West where she understood standards were so much higher. If she could make it there, she could make it anywhere, she reasoned. So she really didn't think about it for another couple of years.

Then they'd placed her in London and she'd gone and met Martin. Beautiful, confident, kind Martin with his reddish hair and clear blue eyes. The faint suggestion of freckles across his nose made him seem at once boyish and harmless. Martin whose attention had confused her at first and later made her feel just ever so slightly superior. She would never have admitted that to anyone of course. A woke worldly woman like her could never see being accepted by white people as some kind of badge of honour. And of course, she hadn't been completely accepted because Martin's mother refused even to meet her. But in the early period of their relationship, in that first year, when they had seemed to be planning a future together, yes, it really had seemed like a certainty. Like their son, Asante, would one day be a real person, a baby.

She had presented the name to Martin as a *fait accompli* –
the easy to spell, easy to pronounce, two syllable name that
was distinctly African, yet painless on the western tongue.
Martin of course agreed wholeheartedly, because his liberal
sensibilities didn't allow him to seem to object, and certainly
not to replace an authentically African name with something
perhaps a little more familiar, like say Andrew or Graeme, or
even Sam. He was going to go all the way with this role, and
so their son Asante, as a concept was born. They could see
themselves as responsible but forward thinking parents,
could picture their Instagram feeds with their cute-as-a-
button, multiracial baby as they holidayed in exotic
locations, or picnicked in the garden of the large airy home
they would buy. They both earned enough to assure them
that it was just a matter of time before those dreams became
reality.

Neither she nor Martin had reckoned the power of
parental influence though. For two years, his mother refused
to meet her. Refused even to acknowledge her presence in
Martin's life, and when the mother became ill, well… it
became too much for Martin, and the tug of war of love had
to be ended. She lost.

And so Asante remained unborn. Then there was the
recovery period and the return home to a Zimbabwe so
changed from the one she had grown up in, her parents so
aged, seemingly overnight, their roles somehow awkwardly
reversed, and the power they had held over her relinquished,

and everything out of kilter and so of course she couldn't have a baby in the middle of all that. There'd been no one to have one with anyway. So she'd focused on recalibrating her career path and re-igniting her love of winning, and that seemed to be fine for a while. She made money, bought a house, and then another, moved out of banking and into venture finance, served on the boards of listed companies, advised government on projects, and generally became the celebrated professional she had set out to be.

Her father was proud, but kept that wary look in his eyes, as if he wanted to say something but thought better of it. Her mother was momentarily satisfied, though she'd murmured to her own sister Mainini Flora, that it was perhaps time her daughter got herself a husband and family. No one said anything directly to her though; they seemed at once to fear and revere her. The girl child who had ticked all the boxes that parents worry about, who had completed her studies without scandal, who had worked hard and acquired the necessary important things, who ensured her parents were enjoying a comfortable old age, who excelled in her career and was never seen in nightclubs or at any of the dodgy parties that successful young women sometimes seem to gravitate towards. She had done everything right; no one could fault her, and so no one dared.

And then after her father had passed and her mother had become ever more fragile and helpless and needy, and her brother Mazvita had married and moved away, and her mother had been depressed and blamed his wife, after all this, she was a little tired. And anyway, she just couldn't seem to meet anybody one could have a serious relationship with, and she was doing well at work and that was fine.

Once Mazvita had started having kids – his wife seemed to pop them out like seeds – she started to think about it again. When she held the downy heads of her new-born nieces and then nephews close to her chest, just under her chin and she inhaled the milky, powdery scent of them, when she saw how engrossed the parents were in the little treasures they had created, she felt she understood why it was important. She started to think seriously about what it might look like to have a baby of her own. She started to remember Asante again and all the stillborn dreams she'd dreamt for him. But there was still time, and work and all of that was still fun, and she could see that the baby thing was also hard work – when they're crying endlessly for no reason, and when they were sick at night and the parents were tired, and when they were just plain irritating or bratty or bad. So she put her head down and got on with what she was getting on with.

After a while she looked up and most of her friends seemed to have married or moved away and others had fallen pregnant, some accidentally and others not so accidentally – and their lives seemed to change. Their conversation points shifted, and she started to feel a little awkward around them, like they were speaking a language she knew but hadn't quite mastered. And people started to treat her singleness and childlessness like problems that needed solving rather than choices that warranted respecting, and then it became easier to stay home – less irritating, less of that mild confusion that was becoming familiar. Her mother needed her anyway, so that was always a good excuse.

The men she was meeting then were all either married or completely unsuitable. Like Bekezela who couldn't get past the idea that she didn't speak a word of isiNdebele even though she'd grown up in Bulawayo, or Henry who lived with his mother and was at her beck and call so much so that he had to be home by seven most evenings. Then there was Solo who was pompous and wore pointy shoes and too much cologne, and Masimba, who used none at all, not even deodorant. She knew she sounded frivolous when she recounted these complaints to Mainini Flora, but when she tried to visualise herself settling down with these men, creating a home, a family, a lifetime of good mornings and good nights, it simply didn't work.

And then one day Angela, her best friend from high school, came to visit and said without meaning to be unkind, that she would never have imagined that of all the girls in their class that she would be the spinster living with her mum in the end. And how funny life was Angela had gone on to say, because those voted most likely to succeed always seemed to fizzle to nothing. Angela with her overweight husband and three dull children, who lived in a dusty mining town and still wore shoes from Bata but somehow felt so much more accomplished. And then Angela had gone back where she came from and she was left alone to think.

But it's not the end anyway, she thought, and the next day she'd made an appointment to see the gynae and they talked about options and freezing of eggs and sperm donors and fertility clinics in Cape Town and all those things, and she'd walked away feeling hopeful and lighter and made a note to block both of Angela's numbers. But she hadn't done anything and now a couple of years had passed and now she felt a little panicky and now there was still no Asante.

She felt tired. When she looked at her life, her big expansive, influential life, her life filled with accolades and admiration, with so much success and influence, with boxes ticked and duties performed, it seemed to have shrunk. Like an old lady, reduced by age and expectation and routine, her life had closed in on itself, as if it was a womb, as if it carried something unborn.

MOTHER & FATHER

It wasn't till I was nineteen years old that my mother told me the truth about my father. She said she needed me to be in a position where I was so disappointed with myself that my disappointment in her would be neutralised. She actually used that exact word – neutralised. It would have been different if I was a girl, she had said. Girls understand other people's pain better it seems. I thought her plan was rather calculating, but… well, that's Saruro Sithole for you.

"I needed you to appreciate what it is to be desperate." She looked at me with no shadow of shame in her eyes. She was wearing an odd expression on her face. It wasn't apologetic – too bold for that – but neither was it the challenging face I had seen her wear when she prepared to go to war in the boardroom. It was a face I had never seen on her before – disengaged, ambivalent. It wasn't a frightening face, but I suddenly felt afraid.

My mother was not a woman you would take lightly at the best of times. Although she had a laugh that could light up a room, she seldom used it. She had a gravitas about her that made everyone sit up a little straighter as soon as she appeared. When I was little, I thought it may have something to do with the high heels she wore to work everyday, but later I realised that the effect carried even when she was barefoot in her dressing gown. She was just that kind of lady. You wouldn't want to mess with her.

All of this made the story she told me about my father, about who my real father was, all the more bewildering.

She said it had been tough marrying into the Sithole family. His mom was a sharp-tongued Ndebele woman who had clear ideas about whom her son should marry, and Mama wasn't it. The woman he should have married was going to be a mild-mannered, light-skinned Nguni girl, young, nubile and biddable with child-bearing hips. Although Sithole was a perfectly respectable Ndebele name, it by no means carried the shine of a Ndiweni, a Mabhena or, please God, an actual Khumalo. These were the kinds of names Mrs Sithole needed her son to bind the Sitholes onto. Names that would elevate the family further in the Ndebele community rankings.

So when my father turned up, not with a MaNdlovu or a MaSibanda, which would have been less than great, not even a MuNyasaland (as they called Malawian immigrants in those days) which would have been bad but possibly acceptable, to bring instead a skinny, over-educated, dark-skinned, undiluted Shona in the form of Saruro Zijena... well! He may as well have declared war on his mother and her dreams. What could have played out as a bit of tribal rivalry turned out to be a lifelong sometimes-worse-than-death sentence for my mother. The litany of reasons for which she was unacceptable was long. It was not negotiable; and it was exacerbated when my mother failed to produce a grandchild for the Sitholes right away.

Two years into her marriage, the golden glow of honeymoon season had worn off and the realities of adult life – a mortgage, two demanding careers, repayment of university loans – were starting to take their toll. Obligatory attendance at events of families with very different cultural practices and priorities didn't help and the two young graduates started to experience a definite lag in their energy for resolving disputes.

Initially, Mama wanted to hold off on having a baby just a little longer. She was doing well at work even then, leapfrogging the corporate ladder first as a junior banker in a commercial bank, and then switching to venture capital where her cool demeanour and sharp mind made her a favourite secret weapon for the firm's partners. They had a much bigger appetite for risk than the bank had had, whose passions sometimes got in the way of good business sense. Mama was sure she would be offered a partnership in the next couple of years and wanted to wait till then to start a family.

But my dad, bless his heart, couldn't withstand the onslaught of his mother's vitriol any longer. He thought a baby would help her soften her attitude towards Saruro and he was right. When I came along, things changed for Mama, and although my arrival derailed her career track somewhat, the peace it purchased for her seemed worth it at the time.

But what no one knew was that dad was in fact, not my biological father. And this is the thing she told me last year – after I was caught being inappropriate with one of the students I was tutoring, a teenage boy who was nowhere near as innocent as he made out. His parents promised me a handcrafted, bespoke version of hell on earth. This is the shame she was finally able to share because my own raw underbelly had become exposed.

Mama had stopped using birth control without telling my father. She had wanted to surprise and delight him. But when nothing happened after a few months, she went to see her gynae, again without telling, because what was the point at that stage? After so many tests and reassurances and appeals to bring her husband with her, Saruro knew what the problem was. She couldn't afford to put her marriage through any more drama, so she turned to religion.

When conventional prayer and fasting failed, she moved on to the sects, the Pentecostals, the charismatics, then the VaPositori. "You need to understand what it means to be desperate, son. Your Mbuya was telling your father to find a new wife every week. I had to do something." I was silent, but she could read the disbelief on my face.

She'd gone to the so-called prophet who had cured so many women of infertility. My mom is smart, so I know she must have done the maths and realised what kind of cure was going on. She must have known when he insisted she come at night, come alone, come dressed only in the white robe that his sect required its members to buy, she must have known then that the cure was not in fact a cure.

Within six weeks of that one visit to the prophet, she delivered a positive pregnancy test to my father. He was surprised and delighted. His mother did soften, and their marriage… well, it never quite recovered, but it did survive.

My mother kept her secret.

And we all lived happily ever after.

Until now.

THE UNWRITTEN

It was the peak of summer, and the air was brittle and dry. The fresh feeling of Jacarandas flowering and gardeners working on brightly coloured suburban plots had been overtaken by the October sun – relentless, unapologetic, infusing everything under its spotlight. Every day, people woke up and wondered when the rains would come and how long they would have to endure. Every day Ingrid woke up and wondered at how the universe worked.

She should never have told him about the rape. She knew that now. She had been afraid that he would react badly, that he wouldn't understand; and that's exactly what was happening now. She could tell from the way he looked at her, the way he spoke to her. He despised her.

How can it be rape if you went back there? And over and over again? She could see from his eyes that he wasn't trying to make sense of it, which would have been something at least. No, he had already made up his mind – tried and convicted her. She shouldn't be surprised that he could not take her part as a victim of a heinous crime. After all, for years he had made her a victim himself. In his own way he had raped her repeatedly, taken away her dignity, her pride, isolated her the very same way, kept her captive – just like Gwinyai had done over the months that he was raping her.

For years she had guarded this ugly secret. A giant scab on her soul.

For the most part, she knew better than to uncover it, than to remember it and revisit the pain. She had known then as she knew now that rape is not something which should ever be talked about, ever reported. She knew it as certainly as she knew her own name. There was nothing to be gained by talking about what had happened.

Well, write your pain then, the counsellor had said when she tried counselling. It will be cathartic. Fancy English words for base human deeds, she'd thought. She understood what the woman meant – she was a writer after all. She also understood that the woman could never understand. No one ever would. She understood that she would always be the one to blame; if not explicitly stated, then certainly it would be implicit in the questions she would be asked. What were you wearing? How much had you been drinking? Can anyone else corroborate your story? She knew that anyone hearing her story, her husband included, would assume she was using it to cover up some regretted sexual encounter. The kinder ones might think she misunderstood the concept of rape. How they could imagine that making up a story about sexual assault, an actual crime, could in some bizarre way be easier than saying, "Ooops I got drunk and slept with so-and-so." was something that baffled Ingrid. How?

As a journalist, she had written stories about all kinds of heinous and alarming events – that's what made news news after all – the more unpleasant the better. When the rape story came in, her editor had thought she would jump at the chance. Feminist vibes all over it. She'd listened to his voice receding over the dull whirring of the ancient ceiling fan in his office and politely declined.

She wasn't a feminist. No one had asked her what her thoughts and feelings were. She understood – it was news, not a feature article or an opinion piece. What she thought about it all actually didn't matter. But that wasn't the only reason she had turned it down.

She hadn't wanted to be a part of the intrusive army of people that made a rape victim repeat her pain over and over again. She had lived her own horror once – and then again with each telling. She couldn't imagine being required to relive it, over and over again, for the police, for the doctor, for the relatives, for a spouse, and now even for a nosy journalist with a deadline to deliver. Never. It would never be her. And she would never explain why she took this position.

Having said no to the story and meant it, she went off and proceeded to work on it anyway. She worked through the heat of that summer, researched it as if she was the one writing it, as if it hadn't been assigned to someone more junior, someone hungrier, angrier than she, as if she would ever contribute something to its eventual publication. She researched this story and so many other stories of women like herself, stories of men too who had fallen victim to sexual violence, and children whose innocence had been stolen. At first she couldn't understand why she was doing that – it was not as if she didn't have enough stories of her own to pursue, enough deadlines to deliberate. But still, she did the extra work, and she learnt more about herself and her own life story in that period than she had done in all the counselling sessions she had ever attended.

She learnt that no matter how carefully she curated her thoughts, papered over her feelings, and planted seeds of attractive achievements over this wound in her life, it would always be there. She learnt that the world was still a horrible place to be a woman, to be young, to be defenceless. She learnt that rape is not a crime of sex, but of power. She learnt that the best way, the only way to preserve her power, to get it back, was not to talk about being raped, not to open herself up to all the queries and the questioning, the blaming and even the self-doubt. She learnt that the love of a man or a mother couldn't protect you from the disgust that came naturally to them when they learnt that you had been violated, that somehow, regardless of how many sexual encounters you may have had, that single, (or as in her case, multiple) one that was taken without your permission, made you somehow less, somehow wrong, somehow complicit in a heinous crime, somehow an object of repulsion and animosity, rather than a candidate for compassion and empathy. She learnt that all of the women's rights groups in the world could never ease the burden of the owner of the story once the rest of the world caught hold of it. No law could protect you from stares and jeers, and aunties telling their nephews that this girl had been spoilt and they should have no more to do with her. No community outreach could mend the ripped fabric of a person who now felt that she was less than she should be, because the people around her saw her as less than she could be.

And because of everything she learnt that blistering October, as petunias wilted in suburban gardens and the carpet of jacaranda blooms in the streets turned to a fine sludge under the pressure of tyres and feet, she knew that her story, like the stories of so many women and men and children who had been violated, would remain largely untold, unspoken, unwritten.

LUMP

The lump was growing.

Because generally, if left unattended, that is what lumps do.

It started to expand and to force water from her eyes when she wasn't looking.

I mean, she would be minding her own business and the water would come. It made her wonder if the lump was made of water. Salt water, like the water in her eyes. It made her feel all quiet on the inside to think about that lump. It was a deep, seeping silence. A silence against words that felt like a silence against oxygen. A silence so she couldn't breathe. Because of the lump.

But that didn't stop the water from coming.

She hated the inconvenience of it. She hated that her son could walk in any time and ask about the water pouring from her eyes. Mommy are you crying, no I am not crying nana, but mommy you have tears in your eyes and your cheeks are all wet, no nana it's just the wind/smoke/sun/book I am reading. She was becoming more and more ingenious at explaining the water. Meanwhile the lump was growing.

From time to time, she was thinking about it deliberately, trying to figure out what the lump was about. Other times she was just telling herself that she had learnt to live with it, even to forget it.

Then she tried yoga and they asked her what are you grieving and she ran out of class and never went back. Ran all the way to her car and even left her shoes behind. She keeps telling herself that one day she will go back. She will go back to pick up her shoes. But really, she would be going back because of the lump. But she knows she will not go back because they will find the lump, the lump she never told them about and they will expose it and then the water in her eyes will be too much. Too much. And she will drown and die from the salt water in her eyes and the lump in her throat and the pain in her chest and the rip in her blouse and the crack in her heart and the wound in her soul and the life in her years and the man in her bed and the child in her arms and the duty, the duty and the whole damn thing. And she does not want to die, she wants to live.

I mean, sometimes I am just there minding my own business and the water will come. I mean sometimes I wonder if the lump is made of water. Salt water like the water in my eyes, I mean. Because the lump I mean.

I think it's choking me.

I think the oxygen is going now.

I think I want to die.

Because the lump.

WORLD WITHOUT YOU

I thought I minded it all.

Minded the mess, and the noise, and the constantly being needed. I thought I minded being "always on" for everyone but me.

A hundred years ago, when I was married to your father and people would ask me why we had no kids, I would say children were noisy and dirty and very expensive. And I was right – you are. I thought I would mind all of that.

But then one day, not suddenly, but sort of abruptly, I wanted nothing more than to be a mum – your mum. I wanted to be loved with that passion that makes two little girls scramble at the front door over who gets to hug me first when I come in from work. And so after four years of marriage, there was Daughter Won, whom I had always thought would be, (should be?) a son. Once I had tasted the sweet delights of daughterness though, once I was immersed in the downy comforts of daughtering, I knew we wouldn't need a boy. And so there was Daughter Too. And cuddles, and dollies, and ribbons, and rubber toys in the bath and nursery food and baby talk and puzzles, and black girl hair things. And all of it was lovely. And all of it was a lot.

And I thought with time I would mind.

I thought I wanted a pristine car, without the scars of early morning rushed reversing, or the debris of your hockey matches and ballet lessons. An organised grown-up person's car, without your abandoned lunch boxes containing half eaten sandwiches you tried to squeeze in between activities and crumpled chocolate wrappers you somehow always found time to savour. A car in which the radio was always tuned to classic FM or the CD in the player was Evita and not Now 69 or Junior Praise and Worship Hits or Barney and Friends.

I thought I wanted quiet evenings with meals that involved seafood and lettuce and dry bubbly drinks and adult company.

I thought I could use a touch more gastronomic complexity in place of the robust quantities of potato wedges and meatballs and custard that you prefer. I thought coming home to long jazz-accompanied bubble baths and white on white decor would be a relief from fighting over who can shower next and those hair brushes that repeatedly make their way from my bathroom to yours, and never in the other direction. I thought a tidy life would suit my sense of order and give me, finally, room to breathe easy, room for luxury and self-indulgence. I thought I would like some space to be sexy and sophisticated like I know I can be but have never quite mastered.

But now I know better.

Now that a life without the chaos and litter that you bring is actually within reach, I know that I prefer this life. This life where I am yelling, "Lights on everywhere!" as I wander through the house switching them off behind you. This life, with its bedroom floors like land mines, with the carnage of bags and books and sports equipment positioned to trip me as I make my way to you. To you, sleeping uncovered on a chilly night; to you, whimpering with a sore throat or a cold. To you, disappointed over the results of a test or performance, or you, elated about selection to the vocal ensemble or the pottery club or first team sports. To you. You, the centre of my world.

What will my world be without its centre? Its crumpled, crazy, cuddlesome centre, without its chaos and confusion and complexity, without its connection and completion?

My world without you. Is not my world.

GOOD GRIEF

My father died a few days before Christmas. I had been saying I needed to go home for a few weeks before that, but for one reason or another hadn't quite got round to it. Christmas was coming anyway and inevitably my children and I would have been going to Bulawayo. When my mother called and said he was in hospital, I knew I had to leave immediately and so I did. It was late at night when she called and I was about 40 km out of Bulawayo. My father had not waited for me to arrive. He had died while I was on my way.

When my mother lost my father, she was not only grieving the loss of her husband and friend. She was grieving the changes that his absence wrought in her life. Suddenly, after five years of managing his daily care, welcoming his community of visitors, providing updates on his condition (though usually the update was that there was no change) the house was silent. There were no more meals to prepare for the patient, no laundry to wash, no one with whom to debate whether he was due a haircut and shave or needed a top up of his meds from the friendly pharmacist. She was mourning not just her marriage, which ended as marriages should, with a parting by death, but also a household from which all purpose seemed to have been removed. When we buried her lover that Boxing Day, we buried a reason, a rhythm, a way of life she could never reclaim. Two losses, not one. We buried Christmas Day as we knew it, because it is forever changed. We lost our patriarch, and we lost our bearings.

One of the first things I learnt when I went to run Africa's oldest hospice was that all change is loss, even when the change is good. It became a filter which I began to apply to multiple areas of my life. It helped me make sense of many things – all change is loss and all losses must be grieved. A few years later, when I met and married a man who wore his manifold layers of loss and grief with a remarkable stoicism, I remembered another lesson I had learnt while at the hospice: that grief is a jagged line graph, never a straight line.

It is not only death that summons grief, but any type of separation or loss. Soon after getting divorced, I found that my children were hyper vigilant about my movements. Where are you going? When will you be back? Who are you going with? Why are you going? It was like living with a jealous lover. Only when I narrated these incidents to my colleague at the hospice did I learn that when children lose one parent, they become deeply anxious for fear of losing the only one they have left. They were not policing me as I thought, but rather, grappling for data that would assure their safety. My heart broke for them then, because even though their father was alive and accessible to them, they were travelling a journey of loss with all its complications and conundrums, its bumpy rides and temporary landings. The mourning rites of their separation from a father they adored were just as valid as mine were when my own father finally died.

One day, I am in Bulawayo for a speaking engagement at the British Council. My topic is "The Future has Arrived", and I am explaining to my mother that the audience might really hate what I am going to say. She is concerned but unsurprised. This lady knows me well. I explain that pain can hold you hostage; that a people can be so attached to their wounds that they can no longer see themselves apart from it; that they can barely remember who they are outside of the pain. I am not just talking about a genocide perpetrated against our tribe shortly after independence, leaving families dismembered, communities in disarray and children growing up with fear as their first and staple food. I am also talking about institutional violence and arrested development in the region. I explain to mother that these are horrible things that have happened to our people, that I acknowledge and respect their pain.

And then I tell her about the pain of other people, and other communities. I describe how bewildered residents in townships in Harare were when bulldozers were sent to demolish their tiny homes. That places of refuge became places of peril; that people who thought they had somehow found solutions to the ever increasing cost of living and "made a plan", as Zimbabweans are known to do, found themselves homeless and planless during an operation dubbed *Murambatsvina*. I remind her of the season during which our country, like a woman reaching maturity but not quite there yet, went to war with its stepchildren, the community of white commercial farmers, and citizens saw yet another season, another version of grief and loss. The losses mainly affected the tiny minority of white people that remained in Zimbabwe, but because those whites had (and still have) a significant control of the economy, the goings on in that community affected us all. They were also employers of hundreds of thousands of farm labourers who, with the land now reclaimed, found themselves jobless, homeless, and again, planless. I remind her that those who invaded too had also been in pain, that independence had not delivered many of the rewards people across the nation had expected and that losses incurred in the war remained unacknowledged; ordinary peoples' heroic efforts unseen and all of the combined grief unmourned. But what does this have to do with innovation and future-making in the city of Bulawayo, you are wondering?

I explain to mother that I do want to talk about the future. I want to talk about innovation, machine learning, artificial intelligence, robotics, and digital technology. But I want to talk about these things in context, in our context as Africans, and in the context of Bulawayo as a community. Our community is defined by many things, including our proud history as a warrior tribe. But we are also defined by our pain.

The trouble is no one has a monopoly on pain. Everyone hurts. The sources of our pain might be different, but we all experience and live with pain. What we do with that pain is what makes us different. I tell her that while I respectfully acknowledge the institutional and individual violence that people in the city have undergone, the stories of violence can't end with suffering, that we can write a better ending, and can learn from other communities that have endured massive assault – the Jews, the Rwandese. I tell her that I am wondering if, instead of letting that pain hold us hostage, instead of lying in wait for apologies that may never come, we could make something beautiful out of our pain. If we could turn our suffering into something sublime.

Grief, when it comes, always seems like a surprise. Even when you are ready to lose someone, as in the case of my father, the impact of that loss is never quite how you imagined. It's messy and unpredictable and silent and loud and angry and sad and carries a glimmer of hope and utter hopelessness all at once. You think, "This is impossible," and "Will I ever be happy again?" and "Why?" and "Why?" and "Why?" again.

And then one day something happens, or nothing happens at all, and you think maybe life can be beautiful again, somehow.

COURAGE

Gogo. Finally, I'm grown. You must have wondered so many times over the years if we would ever get to this place. Finally, we're here. *Ses'khona*!

I am a whole manager, a whole wife, a whole mother to a daughter of my own. Who knew it could be like this? I don't wonder any longer when they will figure out that I don't know everything and throw me out. I no longer live in fear of them throwing me out.

I know now that while I don't know everything, what I do know is enough, adequate, sufficient. What I bring to the party is more that I will consume. And that's enough for me.

I know also, that learning is a lifelong process. That it will only end when I fall into my final sleep.

I know today that when I bring myself to the table, I bring you with me. You, my daughter, my mother and all the mothers before you. I bring the richness of your laughter and the sweetness of your singing, the vivid colour of your rage and the wonder of only some of your talents.

I bring all of this with me because the two pieces of fabric that are your life and my life are woven together in ways that I cannot unpick.

I remember the day I finally learnt to knit. When I mastered that tricky manoeuvre that allows the stitch to hook a length of wool through a hoop from one needle to the next without dropping it... I know the feeling as if it was yesterday. And I can vividly see as if from an aerial view, me sitting in the lounge across from you, napping on the couch. The reason I remember it so well is because by the time I mastered it you had been trying over and over to show me how to do it, and you were exasperated with my persistent demands for help. You eventually escaped to your afternoon nap but I would not let the matter go.

Now that I have persistent daughters of my own, I know exactly the feeling you must have been feeling. I wonder what my mother would have said if she had been here. I wonder if she would have had your patience.

The other day I told my little one that I was very tired and she wondered why. I told her that just being me was a full time job and a very tiring one at that. She seemed to understand.

Remember when you told me the story about mum? About how she was running the Miss Zimbabwe pageant and that year she was in charge of organising Miss Harare? They booked the glamorous Seven Arts Theatre, entertainers, sound, lighting all the usual things. No one came. Well, the crew was there, and so were the contestants. But no one came to watch the show. It was watched only by those who were involved in organising it. She lost a lot of money, and also lost face. That experience hurt a lot. It was like a burn.

But it was not the last event she ever organised.

Then you told me about the time she ran a public Customer Care workshop at St Lucia Park. Of the people who had registered, only one showed up. And so she had to train him – for all four days: flip charts, workbook, group work and all. It was hard. And also embarrassing.

But it was not the last workshop she ever ran.

Then there was the time she had to call it a night on the Masterclass. She said, "I am not bleak with despair and I am not throwing my hands up and saying I won't do this again. I will do it again next month, and even the month after that because I genuinely believe it can work."

Those are the stories I remember from you about my mum. Stories to remind you that life is full of disappointments – in work, in love, in friendships, in projects. It doesn't mean you stop trying. You can't know when to quit and when to keep trying if you are just playing it safe all the time. Yes, falling on your face hurts, especially if people are watching. But is it really worse than the slow death of not taking risks?

Gogo, you were always good to me. But I still miss my mum. Luckily your stories about her helped me learn so many things. She wasn't here for the bulk of my life, but you know, she taught me to build my businesses, call my crushes, launch my projects, write my books, and try new things. Thanks to your stories, I don't worry about the spectators, they'll be watching another show by Friday! I've learnt to be here for my own progress, whatever that looks like.

I'm also here to model everything you and mama taught me for my little girl. I will live it so that she can see that it doesn't kill – even if it hurts. And then she'll have to live it for herself. I'll be here to encourage courage.

WORDS DON'T TEACH

Nhai Kudzwai. What will we tell the children? Yours? Mine? What will we say to them about all the things our parents never talked to us about? Things like sex and love, relationships and power and masturbation. What will we say about infidelity and staying in relationships that don't make sense and leaving and going back and money and divorce? There's so much they need to know, but... What will we say? How will we share our experiences without losing their respect, without letting them think they can be as reckless with their lives and their hearts as we were?

I didn't get it back then. Couldn't figure out why our mothers were always so angry. Like furious was their default setting, man. It was like they woke up every morning and chose violence. But I get it now. I mean, their lives were pretty shitty come to think of it. And they were obviously dealing with a lot of trauma that nobody was acknowledging or helping anyone else to process.

Much as I feel like I have perspective now, I still don't know what to tell our lot.

What do you mean tell them just that?

Oh... you mean start by admitting that we don't know what to tell them? As in, we don't have the answers? To be honest, I think they've figured that bit out by now! We definitely don't come across as having the same kind of clarity and certainty that our parents had. Or maybe they weren't that sure; maybe all that scolding was just covering up for the same terror that we feel today?

Do you remember Kudzi, how your mother used to yell? *Eish*, you could hear her all the way down the road to our house on the corner. She sure did have a voice, and when she was mad... *Tjo*! She didn't hold back on using that instrument!

Anyway, yeah... maybe you're right. Maybe we just start by stating the obvious – we don't have all the answers. But what we do have is our experiences. We have to be clear though, that the experiences are our own, right? Because everyone's experience is so different. And every experience is unique in terms of who it happens to, or with, and the circumstances, the timing... all that.

But will we tell them about the things we are ashamed of too? It is easy to talk about stealing from our mothers' wallets when we were little, but will we talk about abortion and one night stands? Will we admit that at some point we slept with someone's somebody or found ourselves in places we had no business being. How will we explain it, friend? And how will we say I did all this dumb shit, but *wena* don't do it because it's dumb? Oh, but by the way I still turned out ok? They're not gonna buy it, is what I think. They're kind of smart, you know?

Maybe we should just tell them stories. No, man, not like parables, LOL. Now you're reminding me of old Mr Manasa and how he would start evangelising us in the street when we passed his house. No, that's not what I mean.

Hayi wena, I don't mean stories like fables either. I mean our own actual stories, with us in them. Yeees, with our real names, guy. Well, maybe not the names of the other characters, but yes with us in them – us, the way we were. It will be easier to tell them stories. Then we don't have to try and teach them anything, you know. We just tell them the stories and the stories teach whatever they need to teach each child.

As for me, I don't even know if God will trust me with actual children. You're right when you say words don't teach. Where did we learn that anyway? When we tell them stories, it won't be our words we are relying on. It will be the revelation they get from the stories.

Only revelation teaches.

Acknowledgements

Telling stories has been a weapon against boredom, convention, depression, and so much more in my life. I owe my health and happiness to the people that equipped and allowed me to tell stories.

My parents and siblings were my first audiences, and they patiently put up with all my storytelling antics over the years - the books, the mock TV presentations, the fashion shows, the dance routines, the business ideas - all of them clumsy and awkward attempts at self-expression. Thank you for humouring me through it all. I am grateful to the many teachers, friends, mentors and advisors who contributed significantly to helping me develop my skills, imagination and courage.

I particularly want to thank fellow storytellers, Caro Williams, Michelle Hakata and Thamu, the fairy godson. More than anyone (including me) these people believed in my ability to write and in the importance of the stories I would tell, and that is a gift I cherish dearly.

Thank you to the editors at *NewsDay* who gave me my first big break as a columnist and everyone at Alpha Media Holdings who provided the space for my skills to grow. An earlier version of Tears in Matabeleland was published during this time (*NewsDay*, 14 April 2011).

Thank you to Jerry Manyonda who did the first read through of this book and let me know it was OK; and to Barbara Nkala, a literary legend whose detailed feedback gave me the confidence to move forward.

Thank you to Samantha Vazhure and her team at Carnelian Heart for granting me the privilege of calling myself a published author, for your patience and guidance.

To Team Brandbuilder - we're doing the things guys. We're finally doing the things!

To the community of old and new family, friends, followers and other believers in person and online - thank you.

The Babyladies - Nia and Zahra are two phenomenal young women that I have the honour to belong to forever and ever. They continue to challenge, teach and inspire me everyday and I am grateful for their strong, sweet, soft, enduring support. I am in awe of you both. Still.

To my husband Admire, who has been patient and respectful through the process of creating this book and the ones that follow - thank you for giving me what I needed without being asked, and for trusting me with our stories.

About the Author

A member of the royal Khumalo clan from Matabeleland, Thembe Khumalo is a Zimbabwean-born storyteller. She was first published as a columnist in *NewsDay*, at the time the country's largest independent newspaper, in a column called Local Drummer. She went on to write Southern Sister, another weekly column for The Southern Eye. During the COVID-19 pandemic, she released a collection of meditations as an e-booklet called Words for Work. She is currently working on her first novel. Words and Other Weapons is her first compilation in print.

A brand strategist and personal branding coach, Thembe has, over the years, produced large volumes of content on the subjects of corporate communication, personal branding and brand strategy, including hosting a pan-African podcast called Brand to Build on behalf of her consulting firm Brandbuilder Africa.

Born at Mtshabezi Mission in rural Matabeleland, Thembe is a mother of two almost adult daughters. She attended the Dominican Convent in Bulawayo and now lives in Harare with her husband. She holds a BA in Media Studies and an MBA from Africa Leadership University. Learn more at www.thembekhumlo.com or follow her on social media @thembekhumalo

9 781914 287442